Doctors Who Followed Christ

Also by Dan Graves

*Scientists of Faith: Forty-Eight Biographies of
Historic Scientists and Their Christian Faith*

Doctors
Who
Followed
Christ

Thirty-Two Biographies
of Eminent Physicians and
Their Christian Faith

Dan Graves

kregel
PUBLICATIONS

Grand Rapids, MI 49501

Doctors Who Followed Christ: Thirty-Two Biographies of Eminent Physicians and Their Christian Faith

© 1999 by Dan Graves

Published by Kregel Publications, a division of Kregel, Inc., P.O. Box 2607, Grand Rapids, MI 49501. Kregel Publications provides trusted, biblical publications for Christian growth and service. Your comments and suggestions are valued.

For more information about Kregel Publications, visit our web site: www.kregel.com

Cover photos: © PhotoDisc

ISBN 0-8254-2734-7

Printed in the United States of America

1 2 3 4 5 / 03 02 01 00 99

To my nieces,
Ashley, Amanda, Autumn, and Lydia,
each of whom has touched my life in a special way

Contents

Acknowledgments

Some people are a delight to speak with. Ruth White certainly is such a person. Although the long-distance phone charges were astronomical (she lives in Australia, I live in Michigan!), we shared some very pleasant conversations. Ruth went the extra mile in her efforts to provide me with a photograph and information about her late husband, Paul White. She also supplied editorial input. I am in her debt.

I also want to thank a number of other people who contributed to the book:

Doctors Paul and Margaret Brand graciously responded to my request for information about their work. Not only did they provide the fine photograph that appears in the book, but Paul also reviewed the chapter and helped to improve it.

The staff of C. Everett Koop made valuable suggestions for his chapter and sent a photo of this hard-working medical statesman.

Rendle Short, son of Doctor Arthur Rendle Short, supplied a photo of his father.

Finding portraits proved to be the most difficult task in the production phase of the book. I am grateful to Father Nesti of Spiritan for his efforts to help me locate a portrait of Fabiola; unfortunately, that search was unfruitful.

Finally, Steve Barclift, my long-suffering editor at Kregel Publications, endured extensive late changes to the manuscript, and for this I am grateful.

Introduction

Dad's voice took on that hush-hush tone that makes a boy perk up his ears. I listened as he told Mom the tragic news. He had asked the villagers about Waolo, one of the lepers who used to come to our dispensary each week for the sulfa drugs the government provided free of charge. The villagers, he said, had been evasive. Inadvertently Dad learned the truth all the same. Unaware of the progress he had made in learning the Witu language, one of the men spilled the beans to another. They had taken Waolo down to a limestone pit and shoved him in headlong to be rid of him.

I shuddered as Dad gave his account. Again, as on many other occasions since we had come to Papua, I was thankful that I was born in Christian America, where such atrocities were not permitted. In my boyish innocence, I had little notion of the moral changes that were convulsing American society in the 1960s—changes that would abolish the Christian consensus on which our civilization and its medical services rested, changes that would permit us to drift back into pagan indifference or outright cruelty toward the ailing.

As Waolo's story illustrates, the pagan world could be very cruel. It is said that in the Roman world the chronically ill were often flung out of their homes. They were too much of a burden. During plagues they were abandoned, uncared for, as their relatives fled to safety. Christianity, however, brought a new ideal to the world. Monks and nuns, as well as dedicated laymen, risked their lives to tend the ill during plagues. Christians created special places of treatment for the elderly and the chronically ill. But as we move into a post-Christian world, the pagan attitude is again poking out its head. As I write this, for instance, Michigan voters are being asked to decide on a referendum that would allow assisted suicide. In the Netherlands, the elderly already fear their doctors, who have embraced and actually practice euthanasia.

Many of the greatest challenges of our post-Christian society have and will come in the realm of medicine. There, life-and-death decisions are made daily. There the great battles of our generation are being waged. Euthanasia, eugenics, abortion, cloning, triage, genetic tampering, drug abuse, quality-of-life decisions, and human experimentation are among the serious questions of medical ethics that face us. No wonder national governments have sought absolute control in the field of medicine. Those who hold the reins of the health system hold the ultimate power of life itself.

Medicine at its best has been the by-product of Christian ideals. The modern hospital, nursing, the bedside manner, statistical studies, epidemiology, and the myriad techniques and instruments of modern surgery were, for the most part, developed within Christian lands, often by men and women who were committed Christians. Unfortunately, in the recent triumphs of medicine, the Christian spirit has too often waned. If we are not to allow the Christian consensus that formed modern medicine to dissolve away, we need to pause and reflect upon the Christian roots of modern medicine as exemplified in some of its greatest practitioners. This book is written with that goal in mind.

Christ has often been called "the Great Physician." Deeply concerned for the sick, He went about healing them. Although He was not a doctor in the traditional sense of the word, and despite the fact that He did not leave a single recipe for a medication or author a book on the art of healing, He has influenced the course of medicine more than any other historical figure.

His influence was of a different kind than that of Hippocrates (flourished 400 B.C.) or Galen (A.D. 130–200)—names famous in the history of medicine. His was an influence on our attitude toward sickness. Christ healed not with medical treatment as we know it, but by His personal authority through something like "faith healing," a methodology beyond most of His followers, who lacked His spiritual attributes. His achievement was less in creating a methodology that few could imitate than in institutionalizing compassion for the sick. One historian of medicine has said that in creating the church, Christ created a medical institution. Not only was healing a preoccupation with Him; He commanded His followers to make it *their* duty as well. "Heal the sick, raise the dead, cleanse the lepers, cast out demons," He said (Matt. 10:8). He made healing a Christian concern both by example and precept.

Not surprisingly, then, many medical men and women have been attracted to Christ. Luke, one of His first biographers, was a physician. From the earliest days of Christianity, Christians attempted to obey Christ. St. Basil (ca. 329–379) founded hospitals where patients could remain as long as they needed. Fabiola (d. 399) founded the first free hospital in the West that was open to the poor. Cassiodorus (490–ca. 585) urged the monks of the two monasteries he founded at Vivarium to study the medical corpus of Hippocrates and the herb lore of Dioscorides (flourished first century A.D.). When St. Benedict (480–547) founded a monastery in 529, he required his monks to care for the sick and included medical care as an obligation of the Benedictine rule. Two hundred years later, his tradition lived on. The Benedictine abbot and encyclopedist Rabanus Maurus (ca. 776–856) pursued medicine with vigor at Fulda Abbey. The words of Christ remained important to the people of the so-called Dark Ages and the Renaissance. One test by which saints were identified for canonization was their ability to effect miraculous cures.

To judge the art of the Middle Ages, medicine and healing were important considerations. Both were frequent motifs in the art and literature of the period. Medical textbooks of varying merit were written. Hildegard of Bingen (d. 1179) left one example, an encyclopedia of natural sciences and clinical medicine. Along with large doses of mysticism and exorcism, it included shrewd observations and herbal formulas. It was far from modern medicine, although the exorcisms probably had at least as much therapeutic value as does modern psychiatry.

Hospitals are an explicitly Christian institution. Something like them existed in Buddhist regions and in Greece, but they had not been particularly successful. The temples of Aesculapius filled a niche similar to the modern hospital, but they were widely known to practice fraud and to milk their patients' wealth. Serpent motifs dominated their treatment, making their temples anathema to Christians. Buddhist theology had little power to motivate men and women to maintain long-term care for the ailing. Consequently, Buddhist hospitals faltered for lack of support. But as the Christian community became imbued with a sense of obligation to society's less fortunate members, hospitals sprang up. These hospitals successfully perpetuated themselves if for no other reason than that the hospital provided a means to fulfill Christ's commands.

Christian hospitals (however faulty their medical practice) were instituted wherever the gospel went, their funds supplied by the fervor of Christian devotees and their labor by the hands of pious volunteers. It is a matter of note that the same Council of Nicea that gave us the Nicene Creed also handed down a decision that each local church must provide a hospital. Monasteries often provided medical treatment, advice, and even beds. The tradition of Christian volunteerism continues to this day.

Hospitals provided a refuge for the poor, many of whom had nowhere else to go and no one else to care for them. Consequently, Christian hospitals attracted converts from among the feeble and the despised. Julian the Apostate, an emperor of the Roman Empire, observed this and suggested that if paganism were to be kept alive, it must create establishments to rival the Christian hospital.

Christians were responsible for preserving Greek medical knowledge. It is noteworthy that Nestorian Christians carried Greek medical texts to Arab lands when they were exiled from the Eastern empire, and that Nestorians for many centuries, with Persians and Jews, made up the bulk of notable physicians active in Islamic regions. (Nestorians had been ousted from the church over the issue of whether Mary should be called "Mother of God.")

Thanks in part to the Nestorians, at a time when medicine was benighted in a barbarian-conquered Europe that was yielding only slowly to Christ, Arab medicine flourished, adding many new drugs to the pharmacopoeia and a somewhat rational treatment of the sick. Three revered physicians of the Islamic world were Rhazes (841–

926), who traveled the caliphate of Baghdad in search of remedies and was noted for his bedside manner; Avicenna (980–1037), who produced the influential but often erroneous *Canon of Medicine;* and Albucasis (d. ca. 1013), who holds the dubious distinction of introducing cauterization into a number of medical procedures. Cauterizations were necessary because Islam did not allow the living body to be cut.

Christianity forbade the dissection of corpses. However, the prohibition was not a religious tenet but merely an aversion. It was Pope Boniface VIII who prohibited the cutting up of human corpses, but he did so only to end the grisly practice of the Crusaders, who boiled the dead bodies of comrades and sent the bones home for burial. Christians of the Middle Ages were not alone in their aversion to dissection. Islam also rejected the dissection of corpses. In fact, most cultures had taboos against cutting the dead. This prohibition hindered the development of rational anatomy everywhere in the world. Surgeons had to be content with learning about the body from brief peeks into living wounds. One culture that did not forbid cutting was that of Egypt, where embalmers removed internal organs in the process of mummification. Unfortunately, in the stratified society of the Nile, embalming was not a doctor's job. Consequently, surgeons failed to benefit as they might have from the preparation of mummies.

Galen was the most famous anatomist of the ancient world. Arabs and Christians, with their prohibitions against cutting, were forced to rely heavily on him. Galen, however, is believed to have dissected only one complete corpse, that of a drowned man. The rest of his anatomical knowledge came from treating the wounds of gladiators or from animal studies; therefore, his teachings were often in serious error. Christian schools followed him to their detriment, and Christian lands did not finally overcome prejudice against dissection of cadavers until relatively recent times. Throughout the world, other cultures rejected the postmortem examination even into the twentieth century.

If the Arab world assimilated from Christian and Jew the need to provide charitable hospital facilities and a corpus of Greek medical texts, they repaid the loan with interest. Their hospitals sometimes were very enlightened in their practice and stood as a too-often unheeded example to the West. In time, the Arabs restored medical knowledge to Europe. Ironically, the texts that the Nestorians originally brought from the West and preserved in the East were brought back to the West in translation, and they helped foster the rise of a modern rational medical science in such centers as Salerno.

Until that happened, early Christian hospitals were useful as refuges but had little to offer (by today's standards) in the way of practical medicine. Sanitation was generally unknown. Not a few patients contracted infection in the hospital and died as a result of going there. Had the sanitary precautions of the Torah been implemented, much needless death could have been avoided. Christians, interpreting the Hebrews' sanitary code as a manifestation of Jewish ritual (which they thought was not to encumber Christians because they were under grace, not law), paid little attention to Moses' commonsense code of cleanliness. Instead, an unfortunate reliance on amulets, charms, and magic was a constant reminder of the heathen past of the Christian world.

Moses might be ignored, but Christ's commands were another matter. Those *had* to be obeyed. And so Christianity as a medical influence began to shine. Explicit obedience to Christ's words brought about distinct benefits before and after the rise of rational medicine. "Cleanse the lepers," Christ commanded. Two hundred years of Christian efforts along this line virtually wiped out this dread disease in Europe at a time when it remained the scourge of the rest of the world. "Raise the dead," said Christ. Eighteenth-century Quakers took Him at His word and sought methods of resuscitation for victims of drowning and other accidents.

With the coming of the Reformation and the ready availability of the Bible to all people, the commands of Christ became apparent to all, and interest in medical reform revived. It is not surprising, then, that modern medicine is largely post-Reformation in origin, and it would be impossible to understand the work of the great medical innovators—Paré, Sydenham, and Boerhaave—without some knowledge of Christian ideals.

This book largely spans the years from the time of Paré until our own day, showing Christianity's influence on medicine through the lives of select physicians. I have endeavored to present doctors who were genuinely Christian and who demonstrated their faith through their actions and words. As much as possible, I have allowed the doctors to speak of their Christian faith in their own words. Because there are so many ways in which a doctor can contribute to the medical profession, I sought to include individuals who represented different facets of the profession. I also have included a wide range of Christian persuasions. To some extent my choices were opportunistic, directed by the availability of source material.

What can we learn from the stories of Christian physicians? The least we can ask of doctors is that they do no deliberate harm.

However, Christianity goes beyond a negative injunction against committing harm to a positive principle of doing good. It is not enough to avoid evil; one must actively promote righteousness. Studying our predecessors can rekindle in us the flame of compassion and faith that led them to their achievements. The stories in this book are replete with instances in which great Christian doctors positively fostered medical improvements and the welfare of communities. That is the essence of the Christian profession of medicine. If this book can redirect even one doctor toward that aim, it will have served a useful purpose.

As you read, you will encounter names in bold type. These are cross references to doctors who have their own chapters in the book.

1

Luke

(FLOURISHED FIRST CENTURY)

Portrayer of the Great Physician

*Our dear friend Luke, the doctor, and Demas send
greetings. (Colossians 4:14)*

Many doctors have followed Christ, but Luke is the first
of whom we have a record. He is the prototype for all
Christian men and women who have cared deeply
about the suffering of people and tried to alleviate their
misery by imitating Christ as physician. More than a
doctor, Luke was also an evangelist, a close companion
to Paul in his missionary trips, and one of the writers
through whom God gave us an account of Christ's life.
Luke was the only Gentile to author a book of the Bible.

L uke steps quietly out of a mysterious past onto the pages of history and disappears off its pages into a haze of legend. It is as if his face were swathed in a bandage with only his lips and luminous eyes appearing. According to tradition, Luke lived eighty-four years. We have no means of verifying that; bandages mask that sort of detail. All we know with certainty is that Luke left a heritage more lasting than the monuments of Babylon and more solid than the pyramids of Egypt. His lips uttered syllables that reverberate to this day.

Luke probably was born the son of slaves. Tradition says so, and his single, short name supports the tradition. Where or in what circumstances he uttered his first cry, we do not know. Some people believe he was a Macedonian because his narrative, The Acts of the Apostles, gives much attention to the details of Paul's Macedonian ministry. But Luke was an active participant in Paul's work and a good reporter, so it would not be surprising if vivid details crept in, just as they do when he reports Peter's deliverance from prison and other events of particular interest. Other scholars declare that Luke was from Antioch. The early church historian Eusebius left an account to that effect. Of one thing we are sure: Luke came of Hellenic stock. This means he was the only Gentile to author a book of the Bible.

One way out of slavery was to become a doctor. Under the caesars, physicians were honored with Roman citizenship no matter how lowly their birth. All the same, if it is true that Luke was born a slave, we do not know how he afforded medical school. We do know that his studies could have taken place on the island of Cos or at Rhodes or Athens.

Most likely, Luke began his serious studies around the age of fourteen. That was a common age for the commencement of higher education even as late as the nineteenth century. Luke probably learned Latin. Most cultured men of the period spoke at least two languages. Common Greek would have been his native language; Latin was the tongue of the empire. Luke would have studied the Hippocratic works, a collection of medical writings (often contradictory) believed to have been compiled by Hippocrates. He would have recited the Hippocratic Oath, a lofty ideal of medical ethics as

expressed in a doctor's relationship to both his
tients. Luke's compassionate writings indicate
the spirit of the oath, just as he assimilated all that
civilization.

I swear by Apollo the physician and Æsculapius and Hygieia
[Health] and Panacea [All-healing] and all the gods and
goddesses, that, according to my ability and judgment, I will
keep this oath and this stipulation—to reckon him who taught
me this art equally dear to me as my parents, to share my
substance with him, and relieve his necessities if required;
to look upon his offspring in the same footing as my own
brothers, and to teach them this art, if they shall wish to
learn it, without fee or stipulation; and that by precept, lecture and every other mode of instruction, I will impart a
knowledge of my art to my own sons, and those of my teachers, and to disciples bound by a stipulation and oath according to the law of medicine, but to none others. I will follow
that system of regimen which, according to my ability and
judgment, I consider for the benefit of my patients, and abstain from whatever is deleterious and mischievous.

I will give no deadly medicine to anyone if asked, nor
suggest any such counsel; and in like manner I will not give
to a woman a pessary to produce abortion.

With purity and with holiness I will pass my life and practice my art.

Into whatsoever houses I enter, I will go into them for the
benefit of the sick, and will abstain from every voluntary
act of mischief and corruption, and, further, from the ab-
duction of females or males, of freemen and slaves. Whatever, in connection with my professional practice, or not in
connection with it, I see or hear, in the life of men, which
ought not to be spoken of abroad, I will not divulge, as reck-
oning that all such should be kept secret.

While I continue to keep this Oath unviolated, may it be
granted to me to enjoy life and the practice of the art,

espected by all men, in all times! But should I trespass and
violate this Oath, may the reverse be my lot!

At some point, Luke met Paul. Some people think that Paul consulted him about his "thorn in the flesh" (supposing that the thorn
was a disease) or about his eyes, which seemed to have troubled
him. Whatever the manner of their contact, Paul's message moved
the spirit of the younger man, and Paul's energetic love inspired
him. He attached himself to Paul at Troas and traveled with him to
Philippi, after which he seems to have parted with Paul for a time.
Later, he joined Paul at Ephesus and was with him at his arrest in
Jerusalem and through the years when Paul remained in prison and
after his appeal carried him to Rome. Paul called him a coworker.

It was as the loyal companion of Paul, the prisoner, that Luke
sailed to Rome. On the way, they were tossed by a raging storm and
shipwrecked. No life was lost in the breakup of the ship, but Luke,
with the rest of the ship's complement, found himself on the island
of Malta, where the islanders succored them.

> There was an estate nearby that belonged to Publius, the
> chief official of the island. He welcomed us to his home and
> for three days entertained us hospitably. His father was sick
> in bed, suffering from fever and dysentery. Paul went in to
> see him and, after prayer, placed his hands on him and healed
> him. When this had happened, the rest of the sick on the
> island came and were cured. They honored us in many ways
> and when we were ready to sail, they furnished us with the
> supplies we needed. (Acts 28:7–10 NIV)

From these words written by Luke, we can infer that he was modest; there is no mention of himself, only the bare hint of "we" and
"us," although he suffered with Paul in both storm and shipwreck.
All his focus is on Paul, and he gives all the credit to Paul. Indeed,
although Luke was the author of both the gospel that takes his name
and the Acts of the Apostles, he never declares his own name. His
lips always articulate the names of others: Christ, Peter, Philip, and

Paul. We know Luke by name only because Paul mentions him three times in his letters and because many early church writers speak of him as the author of the third gospel and Acts. Several times in Acts, just as in this passage, Luke uses the words "we" and "us" in describing Paul's adventures, showing that he was with Paul at the time. For example, "They honored *us* in many ways . . ." (Acts 28:10).

And why did the Maltese honor "us?" Luke probably helped treat the sick people of Malta. The word translated *cured* often means *were treated.* Luke's medical treatment quite probably was combined with the prayers of his companions. And so the islanders honored not only Paul but also Luke and Aristarchus.

Luke loved Paul and stuck by him. He not only traveled with him and wrote about him but also probably tended him when he was injured or ill. Paul was badly mauled in his journeys and consequently must often have been in need of medical attention. It is fitting that God should have provided the great evangelist with his own private doctor. The gospel would not have gone forward as well as it did if its principal bearer had not been able to continue his task. Luke was fiercely loyal to Paul, remaining with him through his captivity and trial. Much of the book of Acts is focused on Paul.

At times, Luke was the *only* one who remained faithful to Paul. His medical ethic may have been at the root of this faithfulness. If one was to hold the medical teacher "equally dear" with one's parents, how much more the evangelist who had showed him the art of eternal life? Little wonder, then, that Paul in turn called Luke "dear friend."

We know that Luke was a doctor because Paul says so, but we might have guessed it anyhow because his writings reveal an interest in medical detail. Publius's father wasn't just sick; Luke describes him as suffering from fever and dysentery. Luke gives more medical detail and uses more of the medical terms common to Greek literature than do the other New Testament writers. He alone uses the specific medical term *hydropikos* in discussing the man Christ healed of dropsy (see Luke 14:2). In this and other passages, he seems to have wanted to show the precise clinical implications of Christ's miracles, adding details such as "lame from birth," which the other evangelists did not record.

Well educated, Luke imitated the historical methods of Herodotus and Thucydides. They were researchers who undertook lengthy travels to get at truth. In the same manner, Luke carefully sought out the truth, not only making use of previous writings, such as the gospel of Mark, but also visiting Palestine and ferreting out the facts of Christ's life through interviews of living witnesses. When he compiled the material, he opened with a prologue that might have ornamented an earlier Greek history. Commentator William Barclay says that the first four verses of the gospel of Luke are "well-nigh the best Greek in the Bible."

> Many have undertaken to draw up an account of the things that have been fulfilled among us, just as they were handed down to us by those who from the first were eyewitnesses and servants of the word. Therefore, since I myself have carefully investigated everything from the beginning, it seemed good to me to write an orderly account for you, most excellent Theophilus, so that you may know the certainty of the things you have been taught. (Luke 1:1–4)

A century ago, there was doubt that Luke had written the works attributed to him. Scholars even denied that the gospel according to Luke and the Acts of the Apostles were from the pen of the same author. A number of studies, however, overturned their criticism. Today, the single authorship of the gospel and Acts is everywhere accepted. The accuracy of Luke's writing has been widely acknowledged and his authorship generally conceded.

If details of Luke's life are lacking, his character is nonetheless clear. We can ascertain what a person considers valuable from what he or she emphasizes. A writer selects the detail he considers important. Luke emphasized compassion. He alone gave us the parables of the Prodigal Son and the Good Samaritan and the story of the raising to life of the widow's son. More than any other gospel writer, he acknowledged the role of women in Christ's ministry. Scholars have noted that Luke's account is filled with praise and joy. This, too, shows the writer's emphasis. To write of these things, Luke must have been attuned to them.

Luke's career reminds us of the indebtedness Christians owe to pagans. To this day, many doctors recite a derivation of the Hippocratic Oath. The medical ideas of the Greeks were fused with the commands of Christ to create the medicine of the Middle Ages and, eventually, our own medicine.

If Christianity takes a compassionate view toward the sick, and if Christian doctors share a common attitude, Luke helped foster both. His testimony to Christ continues to resound wherever the Scriptures are read, and his ideas are remembered. Fittingly, it is the gospel of Luke that forms the basis of the Jesus-film ministry, which is now so effectively reaching all the cultures of the world. Luke had love of Christ, concern for truth, humility, compassion, culture, evangelical zeal, loyalty, and professional skill. We need seek no better model of the Christian doctor.

2

Fabiola

(DIED CA. 399)

Founder of the First Western European Hospital

*For this reason I say to you, her sins, which are many,
have been forgiven, for she loved much; but he who is
forgiven little, loves little. (Luke 7:47 NASB)*

Christians created the world's first successful hospitals.
To Fabiola goes the credit of creating the first hospital in
the western half of the old Roman Empire. It was imitated by many others during subsequent centuries. The
story of Fabiola and her hospital becomes the prototypi-
cal example of medical care in the early Middle Ages.

It was the misfortune of Fabiola, a matron of Rome, that she had wed a lecher. All Rome talked of her husband's vices, his days and nights in brothels, and his abuse of slave girls. How ashamed his behavior made her. How she averted her lips from his contaminated kisses. His leaden descent into depravity was like a counterweight on a balance, overloading one pan and thrusting Fabiola upward in the other, as a slender, uncorked bottle of perfume, a sweet savor in her corrupt age.

Under Roman law, a woman could divorce her husband. Fabiola availed herself of this civil right and separated herself from her husband's heinous vices. To protect herself, she remarried. This was not an easy decision. She had become a Christian at the age of twenty and knew that by remarrying she would be separated from the church, which considered remarriage to be adultery if a former husband was still alive.

Fabiola's second husband died prematurely. Convinced that she had sinned deeply by attaching herself to him while her first, licentious husband was still alive, Fabiola seized this opportunity to reconcile with the church. Shortly before Easter (the exact year is not known), she presented herself among other penitents before Pope Siricius at the Lateran Basilica and was restored to communion. There would be no half-penny repentance for her. She determined to live such a life as would show all mankind that her sorrow for her irregular second marriage was real and profound.

As a daughter of the Fabians, a Roman family renowned for their military exploits, Fabiola was not without wealth. She immediately obeyed Christ's many injunctions to convert wealth into eternal possessions. Clothing herself in a slave's garb, she broke up her estate and contributed proceeds from its sale to Italian monasteries and the poor. She founded a hospital for the sick, tending them with her own hands and probably even performing simple surgeries. Her role in fostering the Western ideal of medicine is notable. Although Basil had already founded hospitals in the East, Fabiola's was the first Christian public hospital in the West of which we have any record.

That we have this record is owing in part to Jerome. Jerome was among the recipients of her largess, and he did not forget his

benefactress. Writing a letter of eulogy to her friend and relative
Oceanus upon Fabiola's death, he not only justified her remarriage
but also sketched her biography. Jerome was then living at Bethlehem,
where at the request of Pope Damasus, he translated the Scriptures
into Latin, creating the Vulgate, the Bible of the Middle Ages. The
great scholar describes Fabiola's work thus:

> First of all she founded an infirmary and gathered into it
> sufferers from the streets, giving their poor bodies worn with
> sickness and hunger all a nurse's care . . . How often did she
> carry on her own shoulders poor filthy wretches tortured by
> epilepsy! How often did she wash away the purulent matter
> from wounds which others could not even endure to look
> upon! She gave food with her own hand, and even when a
> man was but a breathing corpse, she would moisten his lips
> with drops of water. . . . Rome was not large enough for her
> compassionate kindness. She went from island to island and
> traveled round the Etruscan Sea, and through the Volscian
> province, with its lonely curving bays, where bands of monks
> have taken up their home, bestowing her bounty either in
> person or by the agency of men of holy faith.

Fabiola was of a restless disposition. Unexpectedly, in 395 she
traveled to the Middle East in company with her relative Oceanus to
visit Jerome. Eagerly she devoured Scripture and imbibed Jerome's
explanations of it, as had several prominent women before her. Quick
to learn, she asked him questions he was hard-pressed to answer. At
her request, he prepared two works of biblical scholarship, one on
the symbolism of Aaron's priestly garments, the other on the forty-
two stations of the Israelite passage through the wilderness in the
Exodus. Although she soon became disillusioned with the learned
squabbles of theologians, she respected Jerome and followed at least
some of his advice during her last years.

A threatened incursion of Huns into the Middle East caused her
to return to Rome. At Porto, in cooperation with Pammachius, she
founded a hostel for pilgrims and the sick. For three years she la-

bored in this refuge, which became renowned as far away as Britain. Any sailor or homeless wanderer could obtain succor at this haven before passing on his way.

Her life ended in an untimely death. Her husband's licentiousness had goaded her into a life of charity. Its perfume still lingers. Her death, says Jerome, "brought the peoples of the whole city [of Rome] to attend her funeral. . . . To whom more is forgiven, the same loveth more."

3

Ambroise Paré

(CA. 1510–1590)

First Modern Surgeon

He had compassion on them and healed their sick.
(Matthew 14:14)

Doctors are not always kind to their own. Medical opposition to Lister's discovery of antiseptic surgery and
Jenner's development of vaccination from cowpox
show how bitterly innovation can be met. Paré also suffered persecution from his peers. In his lifetime, he was
scorned for his lowly origins and his use of French ver-
nacular in his writings. Despite this, we remember him
as one of the great innovators in surgery.

In 1536, a young barber's apprentice attached himself to the French army besieging Turin. He was there as a surgeon. In those days, doctors did not perform surgery. That task was beneath their dignity, a task fit only for a lowly barber or his apprentice.

Ambroise Paré, the barber-surgeon, had never seen war. He was deeply moved by the miseries of the common soldiers. "I pitied them," he wrote. *Pity* recurs many times in his empathetic account of his experiences. Through most of history, the art of healing was less art than error, less healing than killing. That situation improved in no small measure due to the compassion of Ambroise Paré. He did not harden himself to the miseries of war, but set out to alleviate its horrors as much as possible, becoming a skilled practitioner in the process.

Paré was without formal training. This was perhaps as well, for experience can teach an observant man better than the errors in books. He had, however, read a little, for he tells us of Jean de Vigo's book *Of Wounds in General.* Nonetheless, it was facts, not theory, that guided him. One night, he ran out of oil of elder with which to cauterize the gunshot wounds of soldiers.

> I was constrained to apply in its place a digestive made of yolk of eggs, oil of roses and turpentine. That night I could not sleep at my ease, fearing by lack of cauterization that I should find the wounded on whom I had failed to put the said oil [of elder] dead or empoisoned, which made me rise very early to visit them, where beyond my hope, I found those upon whom I had put the digestive medicament feeling little pain, and their wounds without inflammation or swelling, having rested fairly well through the night; the others to whom I had applied the said boiling oil, I found feverish, with great pain and swelling about their wounds. Then I resolved with myself never more to burn thus cruelly poor men wounded with gunshot.

Regrettably, Paré's books were not as well read as they should have been. Two hundred years later, uneducated doctors were still using the old, cruel cauterization.

Insight mingles with ignorance in Paré. In one paragraph he has learned to treat gunshot wounds with compassion. In the very next paragraph he tells of a wonderful medicine for treating gunshot wounds that he coaxed from a famous surgeon. It consisted of boiled oil of lilies, newborn pups, earthworms, and turpentine. Paré was consistent, however; he was seeking pragmatic results and thought he had obtained them in both cases.

Paré was egalitarian. He believed in treating the whole human being, whether commoner or noble. Stories of his novel methods abound. When the Duke d'Auret suffered gunshot wounds, Paré insisted that flowers be placed in the sick room to reduce its stench and that the convalescent man be regaled with music, humor, and the sound of artificial rain to quiet his nerves and speed his recovery. The Duke recovered. When a severely wounded soldier was given up by his comrades, Paré obtained permission from the company commander to treat him. That man, too, recovered.

Today, we take for granted that rehabilitation must follow surgery. Few surgeons of that era seemed to consider this rather obvious idea, but Paré did. It was not enough to save a man's life through amputation; he must be enabled to function afterward. To facilitate this end, the kindly doctor developed clever artificial limbs.

Success followed success as Paré wielded his knife. But he did not grow proud. "I dressed him, and God healed him," was his continual refrain. The soldiers he treated appreciated his concern for their welfare. Enemy soldiers once carried him in triumph through the streets on their shoulders after he successfully operated on their comrades. Another time, his own soldiers took up a purse and presented it to him.

Paré fought for truth. Unfortunately, his books, because they were written in French, were scorned by the establishment, which held Latin and Greek to be the only languages sufficiently dignified for discussion of medical ideas. "Hippocrates wrote in his own native tongue," reminded Paré. Despite establishment bias, Paré's writings received considerable distribution, thanks to the printing press.

A doctor named Gourmelen grew jealous. He filed charges of corruption of morals against Paré, invoking an outdated law that required approval by the medical faculty of Paris before publication of any medical book. Gourmelen's suit was watched with interest by the entire medical profession. They, too, resented this upstart barber's apprentice. Given such opposition, Paré was blessed in his friends. The French kings backed him, and he served four of them in succession. This enabled him to survive his opposition. Rivalries die hard, however, and after Paré's death, the reactionary French establishment cast aside his books and reverted to old methods. However, for open-minded doctors, Paré's techniques were a bible of surgery until John Hunter (1728–1793) replaced them with better methods in the eighteenth century.

Far ahead of his day, Paré made many contributions to medicine, including innovations in obstetrics. The ligature to stop bleeding came into common use through his example, as did the surgical truss. His reasoning led him to a vague notion of transmissible infection. Unafraid of censure, he dissected corpses to gain anatomical knowledge. In some cases, he even performed autopsies. He advocated public health measures.

As we have observed, Paré was a great experimenter. He was willing to try old-wives' remedies to see if they might work. Some of them did; some didn't. If he could not always tell the difference, objective observation and experimentation were nonetheless his aims and his greatest contributions to medicine. His ideas about technique and diagnosis fare well after four centuries. Over a number of years, for example, he tested a treatment for burns revealed to him by an old woman, and he showed convincingly that burns treated with her remedy healed without blebs, whereas traditional remedies left unsightly marks.

It appears from several accounts that Paré was a French Calvinist. There is evidence that his family was Huguenot and that a chaplain of that faith was his first teacher. Contemporaries say the king protected his life during the St. Bartholomew's Day Massacre, when Huguenots were killed by the thousands. All of the evidence indicates a genuine believer. We do not find pieties, such as were strewn naturally through his works, in other surgeons' writings. He adjured young surgeons not to work for monetary reward but to do their duty to the end, even in hopeless cases. He was modest, a quality that sprang directly from his profound, unbigoted piety. Not only did he credit God with all of his successes but also his writings breathed a Christlike compassion for all who suffer.

Huguenot or not, he was a merciful man. At the age of eighty, the doughty doctor stopped a religious procession in Paris during a siege and appealed to the archbishop of Lyons not to be stiff-necked but to come to terms with Henry of Navarre. The archbishop unbent, and the siege was lifted a week later, possibly because of Paré's appeal. The point is that his heart was in the right place. Paré died shortly after the siege was raised.

Subsequent generations have revered him. His story is repeated in dozens of collections of medical biography. He stands among the most eminent physicians of all generations.

Thomas Sydenham

(1624–1689)

England's Hippocrates

To one there is given . . . gifts of healing.
(1 Corinthians 12:8–9)

Many doctors contributed to the break with traditions that delivered men from the errors of Hippocrates and Galen. Except perhaps for Paracelsus, none of them took the step all at once. Sydenham was one of the new observers. Although he, too, retained errors of the ancients, he looked afresh at disease. He stands for all those who, after centuries of slavish adherence to tradition, began to observe for themselves.

H istory hangs upon moments. The history of medicine is no exception.

England was at war. Arrayed on the one side were the parliamentary forces representing a largely Puritan constituency. On the other side were King Charles's loyal followers, the Royalists, whose party was espoused by the religious formalists: the Church of England and the Roman Catholic Church. The Sydenhams were not only a prominent family but also ardent Puritans. Thomas Sydenham, like his brothers, rode to war. During that war, an event occurred that might have changed the history of medicine. At a dramatic moment, a drunken royalist entered Thomas's bedroom and aimed a pistol at his chest. The gun fired with a roar. Sydenham stood unhurt. Fortunately for medical science, the soused assassin had accidentally waved his own left hand in front of the gun and shattered that rather than Thomas's heart.

Thomas Sydenham escaped his brush with death to become "the English Hippocrates." But he reached that pinnacle of esteem erratically. He had barely entered Magdalen Hall in 1642, perhaps intending to study medicine, when the war broke out between Parliament and the king. Sydenham's education was disrupted. He was in and out of service at least twice. Once he was left for dead on the field. In a petition he wrote, to obtain back pay owed to a brother killed in battle, he mentions having lost much of his own blood for the cause. In Exeter in 1643, he was taken captive by Royalists and imprisoned for nine months. He could not have had much liking for the Royalists. Not only had one of them tried to take his life but also a Royalist major killed his mother in cold blood the following year.

Riding home from war the first time, Thomas met Dr. Thomas Coxe, who was treating one of Sydenham's wounded brothers. Coxe urged him to study medicine. Rather unenthusiastically, Sydenham agreed, returning to Magdalen Hall in 1647. His studies were scarcely under way before he was made a bachelor of medicine by command of the Earl of Pembroke in 1648. So low were the medical standards that an earl's order could make one a doctor despite lack of training and practice. In practical terms, this meant that Sydenham could serve as an army physician. He remained at the university several years more—years interrupted by his second stint of military duty—before taking up a medical practice in London. Because of his sporadic studies, he did not become acquainted with much of the old and inaccurate medical knowledge existing in books. This circumstance protected him from many errors and forced him to rely upon his own observations and wits, which proved more than equal to the advancement of medicine.

In 1655, the hopeful student set up practice for himself and married on the strength of £600 that Parliament owed his dead brother. He attempted to get himself elected to Parliament. Failing at that, he received a minor appointment called "comptroller of the pipe," which eased his financial concerns sufficiently to permit him to apply himself seriously to his studies. He traveled to Montpellier, France, to attend medical classes. His efforts were rewarded in 1663 with a partial license from the Royal College of Physicians, although he did not become a full doctor until 1676.

Long before then, however, his genius had brought him renown. During the plague of 1665, Sydenham wrote and published his first book, *Methodus curandi febres,* a slender tome that proved highly influential. In those days dozens of diseases went by the single name *fever.* Sydenham, with careful observation, was able to distinguish between a number of them. "In writing . . . such a natural history of diseases, every merely philosophical hypothesis should be set aside, and the manifest and natural phenomena, however minute, should be noted with the utmost exactness." He stressed "peculiar and constant phenomena" common to the same disease no matter in whom it was found. Rather than ascribing disease to an imbalance of a person's "humors," he began to look for and describe the natural history of diseases. Disease might attack a weakness in a person, but ultimately the physician had to fight each disease by methods appropriate to it. Although people differ somewhat in their response to diseases, the diseases are nonetheless distinct entities.

Enough doctors perceived the sense behind Sydenham's new approach that his method dominated eighteenth-century medicine, so much so that the great Dutch physician **Hermann Boerhaave** (1668–1738) was said to remove his hat whenever Sydenham's name was mentioned. Sydenham's clear descriptions of a number of diseases met with immediate acceptance in all of Europe, except among English rivals. More and more doctors began to contribute exact descriptions of specific ailments. When a doctor came to the bedside of a patient, he now attempted first and foremost to make a diagnosis. This remains standard practice.

To the end, Sydenham remained more practical than theoretical. He seemed not to recognize the full implications of his own discoveries. For example, he never completely abandoned the Hippocratic view that disease was caused by humors, a theory that Johannes Baptista van Helmont (1579–1644) had already exploded. For Sydenham, results mattered more than theories, so he could hold to both the old Greeks' theories and his own without any sense of contradiction.

Thomas Willis (1621–1675), a close contemporary, was in some ways more scientific in his approach to medical problems. He moved further away from Hippocrates than did Sydenham, but Sydenham's close observation gave his work on fevers more lasting worth than Willis's similar work. To Sydenham's practicality we owe the introduction of quinine and laudanum into the English pharmacology. Bed rest, fresh air, and diet were the commonsense treatments he preferred to purging, bloodletting, or steam cures.

Among Sydenham's close friends he counted the noble-minded Robert Boyle (1627–1691) and philosopher John Locke (1632–1704). To both he wrote vivid descriptions of the calculus (stones) and gout from which he suffered much. Like these two friends, Sydenham was a Christian, and it is apparent that he had thought out the medical implications of the Incarnation. A fragment of manuscript documents his views. Christ, by becoming man, showed the value of the human body, he taught; therefore, medicine, by healing people, who are in the image of Christ, could and should serve the glory of God. He reminded doctors that they, too, were mortal and would stand accountable before a great Judge for their medical performance.

His sole visible fault seems to have been occasional outbursts of bitterness toward his enemies. Against this weakness, balance his genuine concern for patients, whom he visited personally, sometimes accompanied by Boyle or Locke. He gave real practical assistance to the poor, once going so far as to lend his own horse to an impoverished man who needed riding exercise for his health. He was pious, holding strong Puritan convictions. With the example of Christ before him, he sought earnestly and conscientiously to better the lot of mankind.

History hangs upon moments. We are blessed that Sydenham escaped the bullet of his would-be assassin.

5

Hermann Boerhaave

(1668–1738)

Master of Clinical Instruction

Many are the plans in a man's heart, but it is the
LORD's purpose that prevails. (Proverbs 19:21)

The greatest doctors are teachers. Hermann Boerhaave taught an entire generation of European doctors. Students recognized in him a master they could respect and flocked to him, for, with unceasing diligence, he had mastered not only medicine but also chemistry and botany. His engaging personality enabled him to convey his methods to students in ways that they could imitate. Single-handedly, he did much to create a new, sympathetic breed of doctor.

L ife expectancy for infants was low when Hermann Boerhaave was born. Several of his brothers and sisters were buried before he uttered his first cry. Perhaps this is why the Reverend Jacobus Boerhaave saw to it that his newest son was baptized the day after birth. Hermann survived to grow up a few miles from Leyden, Holland, in the parsonage at Voorhout. His mother died when he was but five years old. Jacobus married Eva du Bois, daughter of a Leyden clergyman. She proved a true friend to her stepson for, even when sons and daughters were born to her, she loved little Hermann as if he had been her own son. Jacobus, a well-educated man, tutored Hermann and set him an example of diligence, hard work, and frugality without which the growing family could not have prospered.

Our interests are formed by events beyond our choosing. So it was with Hermann Boerhaave. At twelve, he developed a painful ulcer on his leg. This sore resisted all treatment and forced him to forgo active pursuits. The problem did not go away. Possibly it was tubercular in nature. After a year, Jacobus determined to send his son to Leyden to study, where he might not only receive better medical attention but also obtain an education that could not be had in Voorhout. Thirteen-year-old Hermann immediately matriculated at the University of Leyden, which he would enter two years later as a divinity student. His ulcer continued to torment him and awakened in him his first flicker of interest in medicine. When all the remedies of the doctors proved useless, he treated himself with a homemade concoction of urine and salt. Inexplicably, the sore went away.

Before Hermann could commence his university studies, however, Jacobus died. The boy's education was jeopardized, for his stepmother was left with nine children and few resources. But fifteen-year-old Hermann won a scholarship, which was made retroactive. This stipend relieved his stepmother of the burden of financing his education.

Jacobus had intended his son for the ministry; therefore, Boerhaave entered the philosophical course that was a prerequisite to his theo-logical studies. Philosophy at that time included not only metaphys-ics and ethics but also natural science. Thus, unknown to him, Boerhaave's feet were planted on the road toward medicine. Over and above his required course work, Boerhaave applied himself to Latin, Greek, and rhetoric. He made such advances that he was selected for public debates at age seventeen and won a gold medal for an oration he offered at twenty-one. He took his doctor of philosophy degree in 1690 (he was then twenty-two) and began work immediately on his theology degree.

Boerhaave was nothing if not diligent. So determined was he to understand his faith and to become the best possible theologian, that he studied the Scriptures in their original languages and set himself the task of reading all the church fathers as a supplement to his formal studies. Scripture alone taught the way to salvation, he asserted. He planned to write a thesis questioning why so many individuals were formerly converted to Christ by illiterate persons and so few in his day by educated divines.

Boerhaave was living at home with his stepmother, who had returned to her native Leyden. In addition to his studies, he began to teach mathematics so as to relieve her of the burden of providing even his minimal support. He also accepted a highly responsible position cataloging a large collection of books recently donated to the University of Leyden. His steady and thorough application to the task brought him to the attention of notable men, and he was recommended for the medical program. As strange as it may seem to us, it was not unreasonable for a ministerial student of those days to study medicine. Ministers, usually the best-educated men in their communities, often dispensed medical advice in the absence of anyone better qualified. With a knowledge of medicine, Hermann Boerhaave would have been even more employable in the eyes of a prospective congregation.

He would never become a minister, however. One of those incidents by which the Lord redirects our steps intervened. Riding a canal boat one day, he spoke one sentence that changed his life and the history of medicine. The Jewish philosopher Spinoza had published heretical works of a deistic nature. Naturally, the pulpits of Holland's Protestant churches attacked them. Aboard the boat, some ignorant fellows were speaking against Spinoza not by the arguments of reason but with *ad hominen* attacks on the philosopher as one who had abandoned God. One man became excited. Tired of the empty talk, Boerhaave challenged the man with a single quiet question: had he ever read Spinoza? The man hadn't. Shamed, he fell silent. Those words were fateful. An onlooker wrote down Boerhaave's name. Rumor spread. Boerhaave was stigmatized as a Spinozist. This charge, of course, was not true. He had even criticized Spinoza in his graduation oration years before. Nonetheless, he now knew that no pulpit would be open to him. He determined to become a physician instead.

Boerhaave completed his medical degree in an amazing two and a half years, graduating not at Leyden but at Hardenwijk, where rates were cheaper. Although he continued his personal scriptural studies after becoming a doctor, his focus was now medicine. He set up a small practice in Leyden, where he worked from his stepmother's house, visiting the few patients who called for him. There was at this time little outward indication of the impact he would have on his chosen vocation. His income came less from medical fees than from tutoring mathematics.

But Boerhaave was never one to waste time. Continuing the pattern that had already asserted itself, he made, in his spare moments, a thorough study of chemistry and the other sciences. His persistence unexpectedly paid off. When the chair of medical lecturer came open at the University of Leyden, eminent men who had noticed his extraordinary scholastic ability approached him about accepting the post, not as a full professor, but as a lecturer. Boerhaave's modesty caused him to hesitate, but he assented eventually. His decision opened the door to worldwide fame.

Years of astute application in every branch of knowledge had filled him with a depth of learning that few men achieve. He brimmed with insight. Students came, listened, and filled notebooks with the lectures on medicine he so easily dispensed. Word got around. Here was a teacher who *knew* something. What was more, he was sociable, open and easy, and of unimpeachable character. Unlike many other learned men, he was quick to give credit to others and never quarreled with even his worst detractors.

Today, we take for granted that doctors will see many actual cases during their internships. Boerhaave was the one who made that a universal practice. He gave bedside lectures in two wards of six beds each, one housing men, the other women. By selecting patients carefully, he ensured that his pupils saw as many interesting cases as possible. And in those little wards he taught his pupils the art of examining patients methodically to diagnose them. If you had asked him, he would have said that his life's work was to establish systematically the functions of the body, assigning appropriate physical and chemical laws to each action. What he was actually creating was a bedside manner and method of diagnosis that became impressed upon all Europe and caused him to be compared with Hippocrates, the father of Greek medicine. He won such a name for himself that a letter addressed by a Chinese Mandarin merely "to the Illustrious Boerhaave, Physician in Europe" reached him.

Boerhaave's methods spread swiftly across Europe in part because of his decision to lecture in Latin, which made him universally accessible, for Latin was still the *lingua franca* of educated Europe. But it was due primarily to his personality. As with any great teacher, his influence was amplified through his pupils, for he taught half of the doctors of Europe, including the soon-to-be-famous **Albrecht Haller** (1708–1777) and Gerard van Sweiten (1700–1772). These two men, in fact, gave us most of the notes we possess of Boerhaave's lectures. From them we learn that his procedure was to visit his patients each day, greeting them with affection and kindness. When a sick person first came to him, he asked questions, recorded a clinical history, examined the state of the patient, and logged that with his diagnosis and prognosis. Each day thereafter, he updated these notes according to the progress of the patient. Senior students were invited to give advice.

Not every doctor in Europe could sit under Boerhaave's lectures, of course. Those who could not, wrote for advice, which he willingly gave. His willingness to serve made him beloved. So beloved was he that church bells once rang to signal his recovery from gout. His popularity was won through his concern for people. The poor, he said, were his best patients because God paid for them. Did not Christ also concentrate His ministry on the poor?

For all his wisdom, Boerhaave's ideas were often wrong. He held a Cartesian mechanistic theory of the body; therefore, he sometimes sought strictly mechanical causes to bodily actions although not everything can ever be explained in terms of tubes and valves. With his views, it is not surprising that he was the first influential doctor to make wide use of the crude thermometers of the day. That was a very practical thing for a mechanist to do and is standard practice today.

But Boerhaave was no die-hard Cartesian. His mechanistic theories were tempered by his refusal to be boxed in by any single theory; he borrowed any idea that seemed to work. One of his chief influences was the innovative English doctor **Thomas Sydenham**, who identified a number of diseases and gave them clear descriptions. (In return, Boerhaave trained the doctors who founded the Edinburgh Medical School, which transformed British practice.) Boerhaave fused medical knowledge into the best synthesis that was then possible. This, too, explains his authority.

More than a doctor, Boerhaave also methodically taught himself botany and chemistry. When Leyden's botany and chemistry professorships came open, he was asked to fill them, too. Thus, for a time, this brilliant and hardworking man held simultaneously three of the five professorships at Leyden—chemistry, botany, and medicine—single-handedly raising the prestige of the university in all three fields. As botanical professor, Boerhaave was in charge of the school's botanical gardens and more than doubled the number of specimens to five thousand, cataloging them so clearly that from a printed list one could tour the entire collection. Aware of the need for an improved nomenclature, he supported the work of Carl Linnaeus (1707–1778), who was giving each plant two names: genus and species.

Boerhaave's accomplishments as a chemist were not without originality; he was the first to isolate urea. His textbook *Elements of Chemistry* gave few general laws. Chemistry had not yet reached that elevation. Nonetheless, it was a good work—clear, readable, and based on personal experience—showing the definite influence of another great innovator, Robert Boyle.

Repeatedly, biographers find evidence of powerful Christian influences in the background of the great men of the West, and this certainly is true of Boerhaave. He became great in part because of his family and his faith. As we have noted, his devout father personally supervised his education. Hermann's mother had been a pious woman. Although he remembered little of her, she undoubtedly influenced his early character. His stepmother had an even greater influence on him, and she also was possessed of deep faith. Boerhaave himself was a student of the Bible until his death.

His character proved the impress of his faith. He was deeply loyal to anyone who had given him a leg up. As an example of Boerhaave's loyalty, he lamented that he had been able to do so little for his stepmother in return for her kindness. To repay his debt to her, he assisted his stepbrothers and stepsisters when it came into his power to do so.

The great Dutch teacher suffered severely from gout and inflammation of the joints in his last days. His pain was severe and lingering, but he did not complain. All of his life he had been cheerful, injecting mirth and good humor into his conversation. As he neared death, he accepted his misery with Christian fortitude: "He that loves God ought to think nothing desirable but what is pleasing to the Supreme Goodness." In this he was like Christ, who put God's will and glory foremost.

He was also like Christ in other ways. As the famed literary critic Samuel Johnson (1709–1784) observed, "His piety, and a religious sense of dependence on God, was the basis of all his virtues, and the principle of his whole conduct." Thus, he was Christlike in his patience. Asked how he could so calmly receive serious provocation, Boerhaave confessed that he was quick-tempered but by daily prayer and meditation had mastered himself. Indeed, his practice was always to spend an hour in prayer and meditation each morning as soon as he rose from bed. He said that this gave him strength for the day. By imitating Christ, he said, he had found tranquillity.

He also imitated his master in forgiving enemies. When a certain Cartesian vilified Boerhaave for rejecting doctrines of that school of philosophy and said that Boerhaave was undermining Christianity (the critic believed that one could be a Christian only if a thorough Cartesian as well!), the authorities of Leyden took action against the man. They would have inflicted more discipline if Boerhaave wished it, but the great doctor replied that he would "think himself sufficiently compensated" if his opponent was let off with the warning he had already received.

Boerhaave's contribution to medicine was not the discovery of a new disease or practical measures to improve some long-standing horror, such as the rate of infant mortality, which continued to be as high as ever. Indeed, all but one of his own children died in infancy. Instead, he taught his successors to record and analyze disease in a manner that, over time, elevated knowledge. Regrettably, few people achieve the spirit of Boerhaave. Most prefer knowledge chiseled in stone. He who had striven so hard to advance medical inquiry would have been saddened to learn that its progress was in many instances retarded by those who were loyal to his memory. They forbade new pupils to vary or update the compilations he left behind, even in light of new knowledge.

6

Albrecht von Haller

(1708–1777)

Universal Genius and Physiologist

Sow your seed in the morning, and at evening let not your hands be idle, for you do not know which will succeed, whether this or that, or whether both will do equally well. (Ecclesiastes 11:6)

In the history of medicine, many comprehensive systems were developed with little foundation in fact. Albrecht von Haller came of a new breed of doctor that sought to establish by experimentation the truth of conclusions. A man of prodigious learning, he is considered the father of neurophysiology. He stands for all doctors who carved out new disciplines.

Albrecht von Haller's family was not wealthy. In his ancestry there were no great geniuses. The family tended to hold low-ranking public offices. Both his mother and his father died while the boy was very young. As if he were destined to begin life with disadvantages, he was also sickly and weak of body. Compounding his difficulties, he was of an irritable temperament and highly introverted, even morose. But such natures sometimes enjoy the compensation of a good mind, as was the case with Albrecht von Haller. He took early to books; wrote biographies; learned Latin, Greek, and Chaldean; and began vast, encyclopedic projects. It became a point of pride with him to outperform his fellow students.

Because Haller showed a religious disposition, his relatives suggested that he become a minister. The family could just as well have suggested he enter the field of literature. In early youth, he had written poetry, an epic on Swiss history, and tragedies. Haller's inclinations, however, were otherwise. At fifteen, he left home for medical school in Tübingen. Tübingen's facilities proved woefully inadequate. For example, the school offered no cadavers to examine in anatomy class. Haller remained only sixteen months at Tübingen before moving on to the better-equipped University of Leyden. Nonetheless, at Tübingen he improved his people skills and shook off the darkest manifestations of his gloomy disposition. While there, he produced an example of the originality that would make him so famous. Using an injection of wax, he proved that a supposed salivary gland in the tongue was actually a blood vessel.

At Leyden, he sat under two of the most famous teachers of the century, the Dutch doctor **Hermann Boerhaave** and the anatomist Bernhard Siegfried Albinus (1697–1770), who revolutionized anatomical texts by incorporating with them a series of inspired drawings. Haller graduated as a physician in 1727. He was a youthful eighteen, a fact that by itself shows the low state of medical practice in those days.

The rest of his graduation year and part of 1728, Haller visited the university centers of Europe and then roamed the Alps. His poetical streak reasserted itself, and his alpine walks bore fruit in a poem "Die Alpen," which is considered a landmark because it was the first German poem to express delight in the beauty of mountain scenes. The idea, common enough now, was thoroughly original then and inaugurated a trend in German poetry.

He had undertaken the mountain tour with the intent of collecting botanical specimens. Haller's lifelong study of alpine botany culminated in an outstanding work on Swiss plants, which developed a classification scheme considered more logical than that of Linnaeus. But this accomplishment was yet in the future. At present, the young man studied mathematics with one of the ten or twenty top mathematicians of all time, Johann Bernoulli I (1667–1748). He also practiced medicine, taught a short course of lectures at Basle, made anatomical investigations, and sought a suitable appointment.

That appointment did not materialize until 1736, when he was invited to teach anatomy, surgery, and medicine at the recently opened University of Göttingen. This broad scope of responsibility was just what his genius required for its fruition. For seventeen years, Haller carried on his duties with such dedication that he made the university famous. He was considered the great medical authority of the day. A story—it may be only legend—says that a pirate boarded an English ship and found a box of books addressed to Haller. The rogue dropped off the books at his next port of call, believing that it would be wrong to rob the hard-working scholar.

Haller produced a six-volume annotation of Boerhaave's lectures, edited an influential journal, contributed numerous articles of his own on a wide range of subjects, produced a faithfully illustrated atlas of blood vessels, and undertook many careful anatomical studies. His view of nature was that it reflected God. "The whole world's structure shows His workmanship," he declared in one of his poems.

Haller was practical as well as poetical. To prove that the thoracic cavity does not contain air, as one rival declared, he simply opened an animal thorax under water and showed that no bubbles emerged. He experimented. In 1747, he published an epochal work, *The First Lines of Physiology,* in which he summarized his findings. The picture he gave of the heart's action, while inferior to Harvey's, was nonetheless original. Although aware of the existence of capillaries, he believed that blood sometimes passes from arteries to veins without traveling through capillaries. He described with thoroughness the vascular system that supplies the bones, accompanying his text with explanatory drawings of the highest caliber. His was the first physiology textbook written.

Later, after he had abruptly left Göttingen, he issued an eight-volume study of physiology that not only traced thoroughly the history of the subject but also brought it up to date with his own experiments. He had conducted 190 experiments on muscle irritability alone! Nerves, not muscles, are the receptors and channels of sensation, he proved. All nerves lead to the brain or the spine. He went on to show that muscles tend to shorten in response to external stimuli and that stimuli reach muscles through the nervous system.

One of his studies had religious implications. He demonstrated that the soul could not live in the blood by showing that a heart could continue beating for a few minutes after it was removed from the body and the blood stream.

Examining birth defects, however, Haller misunderstood gestation. All the same, his studies of fetal development were the first to show the varying tempo of development in the womb.

After he left Göttingen, Haller resided at Bern, where he directed a salt works. Never idle, he contributed to the city's sanitary, orphanage, and school systems. He also codified the common law of Aigle. His wide reading acquainted him with an enormous body of scientific literature, and he issued bibliographies based on that reading. As if this were not enough, he conducted a vast correspondence. Letters addressed to him fill many volumes in the Bern library. He wrote theological studies, apologetic works, and three novels with political themes. The theology and apologetic works argued for the authenticity of biblical revelation and the indispensability of faith as a basis for social morality.

That his Protestant faith was a powerful motivation is evident from his writings. He was Zwinglian and was too acutely aware of his failings to live at ease with himself. Despite his brilliant and extensive work, he felt worthless and suffered periods of dejection. This feeling was due, in part, to his inability to overcome irritability. In politics and religion, he could tolerate no views but his own.

Needless to say, this intolerance led to quarrels with colleagues and needling from those who found him too stiff. For example, Haller rejected the mechanistic theories of René Descartes. He believed that the human body—indeed, all life—was considerably more than a machine. La Mettrie, a famous mechanist of the day, knew this, and gleefully dedicated a book, *Man the Machine,* to him just to prick him in a sensitive spot. Predictably, Haller was infuriated. His irritability sprang in part from perfectionism and in part from illness. He was aware of his faults and deeply rued them.

Haller lamented, "For oh how long has there been no vision of the divine! . . . Miserable prayer without strength or faith! . . . I read in the Bible the story of the suffering Savior, and think at the same time of my plants and other buffooneries!—I feel the nothingness of all the things which men summon up for their consolation. . . ."

Haller had a good bit of the apostle Thomas's pessimism or the apostle Paul's spiritual wrestling as recounted in the seventh chapter of the epistle to the Romans.

Haller outlived two wives but not a third. He had at least eight sons and daughters; others died in infancy. His resilience and hard work overcame all disadvantages and losses to make him a great original of medicine.

John Fothergill

(1712–1780)

Merciful Family Practitioner

Blessed are the merciful, for they will be shown mercy.
(Matthew 5:7)

Fothergill's medical discoveries were not of the first rank. Still, no medical history can ignore him, because his philanthropy, compassion, and opposition to bloodletting have given him a lasting name. He was great in character. He represents the doctor as philanthropist. His philanthropy, despite his best efforts to hide it from public view, was well known to his contemporaries and set an example that impressed many other doctors. The fees he received from wealthy patients he devoted largely to charity. A family practitioner, he was one of the most sought doctors of his day. According to eyewitnesses, he was allowed no rest, even when he traveled on vacation. The following account fleshes out a day in his life as witnesses tell us it was lived.

W orn out with the grind of sixteen-hour days and miles of jounc-
ing about London to visit patients, Dr. John Fothergill headed
for the country for a two-month's rest. As the coach bounced over the
rough roads, he jotted notes and wrote replies to his many correspondents. In just three more days he would reach Lea Hall, the country
house he had bought in the most out-of-the-way place he could find so
he could escape the clamor of London's heavy demands. The carriage
drew to a wayside stop. Passengers disembarked and others boarded.

"Dr. Fothergill, Dr. Fothergill!" A head thrust through the carriage door.

Fothergill turned. Who was this brash fellow?

"Your advice, please, sir." The fellow was evidently an apoth-
ecary, snatching a free consultation with London's most famous
doctor. Courteously, John listened and answered the man's question. As the coach rolled out, John dropped his eyes to his writing.
Before he could form a single line, however, he was interrupted.

"I call this positively providential that we should meet like this,
Dr. Fothergill," gushed a woman who had just boarded. Immediately, in front of the other passengers, she poured out a recitation of
complaints that had long bothered her. What did the doctor suggest?

John rested his pen a moment and prescribed a diet. "You are
eating too much meat and rich food," he warned. He returned to his
writing.

"Hmpf," muttered the woman to a neighbor. "He didn't even *think*
about his answer."

John Fothergill flashed a quick glance at her. But with the wisdom of one who has long practiced restraint, he did not retort that he
had seen so many cases like hers, no reflection was needed. Fothergill
might seem a little too "perpendicular" to his contemporaries, but
he was definitely wise.

He began to pen some observations on a recent epidemic of influ-
enza. He wanted very much to get these thoughts down on paper.
For fifteen minutes he wrote. The coach drew to a stop. John
Fothergill dismounted to stretch his long legs. There was a great
crowd at the station, men and women in tatters, fingernails dirty and
broken with toil. "Dr. Fothergill! Dr. Fothergill!" cried voices.

"Please, sir, my daughter," cried one.

"Sir, help me!" shouted a man with a hoarse voice.

"For God's sake, have mercy," came another plea.

Inwardly, John sighed a little, but he let no one see his dismay. Turning briskly to the coachman, he said, "Put off my bags. I'll catch the next coach." Although an introvert, he loved people with a genuine compassion. His heart was moved by these tattered country folk, the working classes of England, who labored so hard for so little. "Bring me a table," he said.

Seating himself behind the table, he examined the poor country folk one by one. Somehow, they had learned that he was traveling up country and had gathered from miles around in the desperate hope that he might be able to suggest some remedy for ills no one else could cure.

For hours, John listened and prescribed. He gave his diagnoses and instructions swiftly in a voice that rang with the authority of long practice.

A widow stood before him. Perhaps she was thirty, but poverty and hard work made her look fifty. What she needed was rich broth of meat and a fortnight's rest, he knew; but he also knew that she could not afford either. He wrote her a prescription and reached into his bag, bringing out a little box. "Take this home," he said. "It has a medicine that will help you. Be sure to follow the instructions I have written." He smiled with secret joy. When she opened the box, she would find in it not only a prescription but also a golden guinea, which would buy her the food she needed. Seeing his smile, she smiled in return.

"Thank you, sir." Hope shone on her face.

The next case, a fair-haired girl, was a sad sight. Her father carried the frail body as easily as a rag doll. Fothergill noted in the father's clothes and the girl's callused hands the evidences of poverty. The girl looked at him with bright, frightened eyes.

"Am I going to die?" she whispered.

Fothergill took her hand and stroked it kindly before lifting her eyelids. He did not really need to examine the girl. Her case was clear to him at once. She had consumption (tuberculosis) aggravated by weak blood (anemia). What she needed most was sunshine, rest, and sea air. Judging from the marks on her arms, she had been bled. When would doctors cease this foolish practice? A doctor should support the body's struggle for life rather than weaken its resistance through old-fashioned and useless treatments. Yes, the girl's problem was instantly clear. If he examined her more thoroughly than he needed, it was so that he might have a pretext to assist this family without embarrassing the father's pride.

Fothergill beckoned the man around the table and spoke into his ear in a low voice. "This is a very interesting case. It has been of great value to me to examine your daughter. I am in your debt. Accept this token of my appreciation." He pressed five pounds into the man's hand as he issued instructions for the girl's treatment. There was *not* to be any more bloodletting in her case, he emphasized.

And so the afternoon went. Some patients were quarrelsome. Others could not comprehend simple instructions. In each case, Fothergill repeated his advice patiently, sometimes two or three times, until he was sure the patient understood it. A very few offered him a little payment. He brushed it aside. "I never accept payment when on vacation," he said.

At last, he boarded the next coach north. He would be glad when he reached Lea Hall. There at least he could expect peace, except for the one day a week when he made a four-mile excursion to Middlewich to treat poor patients for free.

As the stars emerged, Fothergill leaned back. Beneath his neat, white medical wig, his thoughts raced. The colonies in America would soon be at blows with England. It was a shame that the government had not taken his advice to make a just and lasting peace while it was still possible. Men of good will on both sides of the Atlantic had hoped for it—men such as Benjamin Franklin and himself, both of whom were associated with the Society of Friends, better known as the Quakers. Would war cut off the supply of exotic plants and shrubs he had come to rely on John Bartram to send him?

Well, he still had his agents in Asia. How delighted he had been to obtain a tea tree, the first in England. He would miss his thirty-five acres of gardens these two months, but then, had he not usually had to view them by lamplight in the dark after his medical rounds anyhow?

Botany was only one of his many interests outside medicine. Another interest was Benjamin Franklin's research into electricity. Fothergill still felt a special delight for the role he had played in underwriting the cost of publication of those papers. Consequently, the Royal Society made Franklin a member. Even now, scientists were replicating and extending Franklin's discoveries.

He would write Franklin again. Perhaps they could yet find a formula for reconciling Britain and her colonies. It would be good if they could see each other again. How much they had found to discuss during Franklin's last visit: prison reform; abolition; libraries; and the best methods of advancing science, educating youngsters, and raising medical standards. Fothergill had shared his disappointment that London authorities would not open new thoroughfares to make the city more accessible, as Philadelphia, his good friend's home, had done.

Franklin said openly of Fothergill, "I can hardly conceive that a better man has existed." Franklin went on to add that Fothergill deserved the "esteem and veneration of all mankind." Perhaps Franklin's heart burned with generous anger on behalf of his doctor friend, for despite Fothergill's high repute and evident insight, the Royal College of Physicians refused him a fellowship because he was not a graduate of Oxford or Cambridge. Professional jealousy was at the root of this slight. Fothergill had taken his degree at the new medical school in Edinburgh (one of the first doctors to do so). Edinburgh's medical faculty consisted entirely of men trained by the famed Dutchman **Hermann Boerhaave**, who had helped break the shackles of centuries of cruel medical stupidity.

If Fothergill's bedside manner was acquired secondhand from Boerhaave, his study of disease was in the recent tradition of **Thomas Sydenham**. Like the great British doctor of the previous century, Fothergill isolated and described diseases, writing reports of facial neuralgia (a tic), megrim (a sick headache), scarlatina (a throat infection), and metal poisoning.

Fothergill's exclusion from the Royal College of Physicians did not cause him to lower his high standards for the medical profession. His own medical friends were men of the highest stamp. Thomas Dimsdale, a successful vaccinator with live smallpox virus, and **John Coakley Lettsom**, founder of the London Medical Society, were themselves Quakers. They shared Fothergill's deepest confidence and respect and were frequent correspondents with him.

One Quaker, however, a fellow graduate of Edinburgh, had no share in Fothergill's esteem. Samuel Leeds was an "illiterate" ignoramus whose continued practice of medicine jeopardized patients, and Fothergill opposed him. Leeds took the case to a Quaker tribunal. There was then no standard by which to judge such cases. This committee, ignorant of medicine, looked at the matter strictly from the point of view of gentlemanly conduct and thought that Fothergill had been overbearing. They ordered the doctor to pay Leeds £500.

Fothergill had from his youngest days sought to follow God's will. Now he searched his conscience and decided he must refuse to pay. Lives were jeopardized by Leeds's quackery.

Leeds threatened to take him to court. To protect himself, Fothergill entered a plea. The Quakers thought that this was wrong because one Christian would be going to court against another Christian. After many months of wrangling that caused Fothergill deep distress, the case was heard. The judge ruled that Fothergill had merely done his duty. Leeds died the following year, impoverished. His wants were supplied at the end by an anonymous hand. Such was Fothergill's reputation for secret charity that it was widely rumored that he was Leeds's secret benefactor.

Fothergill was an active participant in his church. A leading figure in Quaker assemblies, he labored to restore the purity of Quaker society. As he wrote to the notable chemist Joseph Priestly, whom he had often assisted with financial gifts, "It is my fervent wish that all the professors of Christianity may be more anxious to live Christian lives. . . ."

According to Fothergill's definition, a Christian was one who served his neighbor. If he saw a need, he strove to meet it. Thus, he was active in forming a society to promote methods of what we would call first-aid resuscitation. He actively lobbied for the widening of London's streets and the creation of new streets. When John Woolman, the scrupulous Quaker abolitionist, visited England, Fothergill received him and supported the cause. He advocated a better system of recording vital statistics, with special emphasis on the causes of deaths. He joined forces with John Howard to obtain prison reform and testified before the House of Commons on the topic. Recognizing the worth of education, he helped found a Quaker school, which, he was pleased to report, soon had one hundred fifty male and eighty female students. He sponsored the poor scholar Anthony Purver, who was making a more accurate translation of the Bible.

After an abstemious and healthy life, Fothergill contracted a tumor of the prostate that quickly proved fatal. As he approached eternity, he spent time with his dearest friend, David Barclay, an eminent Quaker theologian. Barclay reported that Fothergill was serene in his last illness, convinced that he had not lived in vain but had set aside personal considerations to help his fellow men.

To his beloved sister Ann, who was by him, Fothergill said, "[B]e content. Do not hold me. I have been low. I have been doubtful whether it would be well with me or not, but now I am satisfied beyond a doubt—beyond a doubt, that I shall be everlastingly happy. My troubles are ended, therefore be content, and mayst thou be blessed in time and in eternity."

His last two weeks he spent in great misery, and he died the day after Christmas, 1780. If ever a man practiced both medicine and faith, that man was Fothergill.

8

James Ramsay

(1733–1789)

Abolitionist Surgeon

Blessed is he who has regard for the weak; the LORD delivers him in times of trouble. The LORD will protect him and preserve his life. . . . The LORD will sustain him on his sickbed and restore him from his bed of illness.
(Psalm 41:1–3)

We have in James Ramsay an example of the doctor as reformer. Doctors (like pastors, politicians, and lawyers) continually come into contact with people in their most desperate hours of human need. To James Ramsay's credit, he sought the betterment of the most despised class of all, the slaves of the West Indies.

James Ramsay dipped his quill pen into the inkwell. In spite of himself, a shiver of dread touched his heart. *They'll hammer me with all they've got,* he thought. His next line was almost a plea for mercy. "My intention is to convince and conciliate, not to inflame," he wrote.

It will be St. Kitts all over, he thought as he blotted what he had written. For twenty years he had endured the anger and spite of St. Kitts's slaveholders. Threatened with assassination, denounced at his own communion altar, and ostracized by his neighbors, Ramsay had finally wearied of the struggle and returned to England. Even now, however, the shocking sights and sounds of the slave trade would give him no peace. Knowing full well what he must face in abuse, he had taken pen to paper and poured out this lengthy "Essay on the Treatment and Conversion of Slaves in the British Sugar Colonies."

With a surge of defiance, Ramsay rose to his feet. Let the slave interests do their worst! His conscience would be clear. He picked up the paper and headed to the door. He would take this to the printer now.

Ramsay's paper is rightly considered the first salvo in the campaign that abolished slavery. Kind, plucky surgeon-pastor James Ramsay paid for his protest with both his health and his life.

Ramsay knew about slavery both as a doctor and as a pastor. As a young man, he had wanted to become a minister. His devout mother was all for this plan, but his father was not. Ramsay compromised: he apprenticed himself to Dr. Findlay of Fraserburgh (that was how one became a doctor in those days) but at the same time took classes toward a master of arts degree, which would permit him to enter the church. During his first term at school, he barely subsisted, for he had a scholarship of only £5 per year. But this amount was increased after the holidays. Doctor Findlay entrusted him with full responsibility for a "hopeless" case in which a woman had been viciously gored by a bull. Ramsay's skillful, persistent care saved her life and brought him to the attention of authorities. His stipend was increased to £15 a year, an amount on which he could thrive.

For two years, beginning in 1755, he practiced medicine and gained more experience with Dr. Macaulay of London. Thereafter, he joined the navy as an assistant surgeon. He was fortunate to sail under Captain Charles Middleton, an evangelical Christian, on the *Arundel.* This ship saw a good deal of action, and James showed himself brave and compassionate. Middleton became his lifelong friend and sponsor. The seamen grew to love him for his kindness.

On November 20, 1759, the *Arundel* overtook the *Swift* of Bristol. That day changed Ramsay's life.

The *Swift* was a slave ship. Her cargo of human misery lay chained together below decks in a low, suffocating hold. Plague had broken out. When none of the other doctors would venture aboard the *Swift,* fearing to contract the plague, Ramsay showed the courage that marked his whole life. He volunteered to go aboard.

If the *Swift*'s captain was like many others, he cared nothing for the Africans he hauled, except as potential sales. He also cared little for his crew. Many captains were glad to see crew members die once the coast of Africa was left behind. It meant that they did not have to be paid their shares, and more profits could go to the survivors. But the captain did not want to lose his valuable cargo of bodies. Every dead slave was a direct loss for the market in the islands.

As Ramsay stepped aboard, a foul stench assaulted his nostrils. He could barely force himself to descend into the bowels of the ship to examine the sick. Overcoming his sensibilities, however, he did, and was moved by the sight of these victims—packed like sardines; naked; wallowing in one another's blood, feces, and vomit; gasping for air in the hot, oxygen-depleted hold—so wretched that they longed only for death. He gave the best directions he could for their care and left medicines. Then he returned to his ship, vowing to do something to ameliorate the condition of slaves.

He had no idea what he, a lowly surgeon, could do. But God knew. Ramsay needed more education on the problem. He needed to work among the slaves and learn their conditions. It seems providential that, as Ramsay came back aboard the *Arundel,* he slipped and broke his thigh. Fearful of further falls, because of the pronounced limp that resulted from that accident, Ramsay decided to leave the navy. He would live on one of the islands.

Without his knowledge, friends made arrangements for him to

become a partner in a lucrative medical practice. But Ramsay rejected the offer; he had ideas of his own. St. Christopher's Island (St. Kitts) needed Church of England clergymen. He determined to take holy orders. In 1762, he sailed with Sir Charles to England, where he was ordained. Back on St. Kitts, he commenced work for both planter and black slave.

He threw open the church at certain hours for the slaves, urged their masters to lead them in prayers before and after work, drew up lessons for the slaves, and prayed publicly for their conversion.

This last act estranged his congregation. Many quit attending services. They resisted any effort to convert their slaves to Christ. Ramsay had married a planter's daughter and was rearing a family. To protect his family from threatened violence, he had to drop public prayers for the salvation of slaves from his church service.

He was overstepping his bounds, murmured his congregation. He was a "pushy" parson, and pushy parsons did not get on well in the Indies. Most parsons had learned to step back, take it easy, and hobnob with the planters. What right did he have to meddle with their affairs?

When Ramsay dared to side against an attempt by the big planters to gouge the rest of the island's inhabitants with a change in interest rates, he became even more vilified. He spent a large portion of his savings fighting the interest rate law for he saw clearly that a few rich men would profit while the rest of the islanders would suffer ruin. Although he saved the island's economy, he received no thanks. He was stripped of his role as a magistrate. Newspapers heaped scorn on him. Men who could not write picked quarrels with him to ingratiate themselves with his powerful enemies. "To do him injury was an act of valor," wrote one biographer. He was ostracized. His enemies tried to cut his salary. They blocked his raise. A fellow named Gillard stood at the communion table and bawled abusive words and foul language at Ramsay for an hour and a half. Ramsay was without recourse.

Ramsay's enemies thought they would injure him by forcing more duties on him. He said he would gladly accept any duties. They sneered that he was unfit to preach to white people; they should send him slaves. He replied that the soul of the poorest black man was of inestimable value and he would gladly preach to him.

With little to do at church, James Ramsay did not sit idle. He became doctor to the slaves of several nearby plantations. As doctor, he observed and treated the appalling abuse of humans by humans. The slightest infraction by a slave could result in vicious reprisals. Cruel overseers were known to mash slaves' bones with sledgehammers and to whip them until their backs lay open and bloody. Burning was not unknown.

If the wanton cruelty was atrocious, neglect accounted for even more misery. Slaves were inadequately fed. Consequently, they suffered diseases of malnutrition. They were forced to work such long hours tending cane mills that they dozed off and suffered severe injuries. Hatchets were kept handy to cut off any hand that strayed into the gears of the pulping machines. There were no other release mechanisms.

In 1777, Ramsay decided to leave St. Kitts for a time. He hoped that, in his absence, tempers would cool. He sailed with his family to England. In England, he hunted up every person who had helped his mother in her old age or who had assisted him when he was growing up and rewarded each.

A year later, he went back to sea, this time as a chaplain. Observing the need of sailors for guidance, he prepared a book on the duties of officers, which was warmly praised. He prepared a number of sermons for seamen, which he later published. He wrote a book on flag signals, which reduced the number of flags needed to signal any action. Ramsay was present at many naval engagements. After a victory at St. Eustatius, he spoke up for a number of Jews who were stripped of their clothes and other possessions and ordered into exile for no other reason than their race. They were reprieved.

Finding opposition at St. Kitts as great as ever, he accepted a living in England. Great was the rejoicing of St. Kitts's planters when he resigned their church in 1781. They would not have rejoiced had they foreseen the future.

Ramsay very naturally shared the story of his experiences with his friends. They urged him to write a book, but at first he was reluctant. Finally, they persuaded him.

Shortly before the book was released, Bishop Beilby Porteus of

Chester preached a sermon against the slave trade, using details provided by Ramsay. He announced Ramsay's forthcoming book. The sermon woke England's conscience. Ramsay's book was a sensation the moment it left the press in 1784. Prominent reviewers praised it. The abolition movement was born.

As Ramsay had feared, the planters pulled out every stop in attacking him. On St. Kitts they had threatened his life. Although he was now in England, they threatened him again, and such threats were not idle. A few years later, one pastor was thrown into prison for opposing the slave trade. He died there. Another pastor's house was burned; he and his wife barely escaped to safety. The planters not only threatened Ramsay's life but also charged him with every kind of villainy: he had been a cruel slave-owner himself; he had neglected his parish; he had tried to incite slaves to revolt; he had practiced simony, the buying of church office.

For a year, Ramsay defended himself almost alone. He had to answer charge after charge so that his foes would not be victorious. The strain took its toll. He developed severe stomach pain and began coughing up blood. Despite his worsening health, he gave his time unstintingly to the good of his parishioners and the war against slavery. Prime Minister Pitt, the reformer William Wilberforce, and others consulted him and drew from him the ammunition for their campaign to abolish slavery. For four years, Ramsay answered charges and continued to publish books against slavery.

In 1789, he published *An Address to the Publick, on the Proposed Bill for the Abolition of the Slave Trade.* Molineux, a member of Parliament who had been bought by the slave interests, rose and viciously attacked Ramsay's character in the House of Commons. Faced with this latest onslaught, Ramsay's health worsened. Two months later, Molineux was able to write in triumph, "Ramsay is dead—I have killed him."

Molineux's triumph, however, was short lived. The slave trade was soon abolished. Eventually, all slaves within British territory were emancipated. Ramsay's life and sufferings were not in vain.

9

John Coakley Lettsom

(1744–1815)

Founder of the London Medical Society

Do to others what you would have them do to you.
(Matthew 7:12)

The private association, whether philanthropic or educational, is a phenomenon of the Christian world. Such associations are a natural offspring of the church, on which they were modeled. It is impossible for us to imagine medicine without such entities as medical associations. John Coakley Lettsom was the prime mover in the formation of the London Medical Society and a key player in other important associations. He stands for the doctor as founder and member of a medical or scientific society or association.

In 1767, John Coakley Lettsom had to drop out of medical school for lack of money. Born to Quaker parents in the West Indies, he had sailed to England, studied in a Quaker school, served five years' apprenticeship to Dr. Abraham Sutcliff, and "walked the rounds" another year at St. Thomas's Hospital in London as the protégé of another Quaker, the eminent **John Fothergill**.

Now Lettsom felt the pinch of inadequate finances. Determined to obtain more medical training but in need of funds, he returned to the Indies to set affairs right on his late father's estate. He hoped by doing so to squeeze out enough money to continue his education. Instead, he found matters in confusion. He might still have remedied the situation and laid hands on a considerable sum of money by selling the few slaves he inherited, but Fothergill had taught him that slavery was a detestable evil. With impulsive generosity, Lettsom freed his slaves, leaving himself penniless at the young age of twenty-three.

> When I came of age the only property I possessed was a little land and some slaves. To the latter I gave freedom when I had not £50 besides in the world. I never repented this sacrifice. Indeed Heaven has cancelled it long ago, by refunding innumerable unmerited blessings, and what I estimate still more gratefully, a heart to diffuse them.
>
> I did not liberate my slaves from any advice of our Society [The Quakers]. I do not say it was from religious motives, merely as such. I had early read much. I had considered the tenets of different religions and professions, and I thought there was only one true religion, consisting in doing unto others, as we wished that others should do unto us. . . . I hope to die in this religion, not having yet found a better.

Lettsom, however, was not without resources. He had himself. He had his education. By the standards of the Indies, he was a well-educated physician. He offered his services to the planters and their slaves. Gifted, volatile, friendly, he attracted many clients and within a few months had amassed the large sum of £2,000. He gave half to his mother and sailed back to London with the rest. On the strength of his half, he attended six months at Edinburgh's fine medical school. To take his degree at Edinburgh, Lettsom would have had to study another eighteen months. Impatient, he sailed to Leyden, where he obtained an M.D. degree the following year.

After that, things moved quickly for him. He became licensed through the Royal College of Physicians, married, and opened England's first general dispensary for the poor. Some ideas are simply right for their times. The dispensary was an immediate success. Hospitals did not then have the outpatient departments now so common. Lettsom's dispensary provided the poor with a sorely needed service. It was widely imitated. Within thirty years, forty of them existed in Britain.

Lettsom, always on the alert for ways to improve the medical profession, recognized the dispensaries' potential for medical education. Since a wide range of cases were treated at these dispensaries, he urged that they be authorized to train medical students and even proposed a syllabus. Eventually, his idea won acceptance, and generations of medical students gained valuable experience through dispensary work.

The brilliant Creole doctor grasped the value of medical associations. A strong medical society would be of value to physicians for apprising them of the latest foreign medical advances. It could allow them to exchange their own ideas and provide a library of medical literature far beyond the resources of any individual practitioner. Medical discoveries could be rewarded and papers published under its auspices.

Several feeble, cliquish medical societies existed in London in Lettsom's day. He studied their weaknesses and concluded that to be viable a society must include each of the three principle divisions of doctors: physicians, surgeons, and apothecaries. He sold the idea of a new society to his friends, and the London Medical Society was born. It is the only such society to survive from Lettsom's day to ours. That it has done so is owing to his tireless efforts to make it succeed. Its success was partly attributable to the fact it was the first "democratic" medical society, serving the entire medical profession rather than the interests of a small coterie of think-alikes.

Lettsom was a Quaker. Quakers had an impact on society completely out of proportion to their small numbers because they attempted to obey the Scriptures, often at serious personal cost. Quakers continually worked for the reform of public abuses. Not infrequently, they succeeded. Lettsom made his own contributions to this noble heritage. He tossed off numerous tracts, called "hints," almost all of which made good suggestions and some of which actually resulted in change. Having found his medical practice highly lucrative, he gave generously to the causes for which he wrote.

Among Lettsom's active pursuits was prison reform. He advocated disinfecting Newgate and introduced to the public James Neild's scathing report on the state of prisons. Wanting to bring the benefits of bathing to London's poor children, he purchased two acres and founded the institution that evolved into the Royal Sea Bathing Hospital. It has been widely imitated.

When **Edward Jenner** was under attack for smallpox inoculation, Lettsom championed the beleaguered vaccinator and convinced not a few skeptical doctors to adopt Jenner's methods. He was mocked for his efforts to introduce mangel-wurzel root (beet) to England. Today, tens of thousands of acres of the crop are planted.

Ever a proponent of associations, Lettsom joined the Royal Humane Society. He attended its first meeting, and he was undaunted by the ridicule of opponents who mocked its efforts to advance first aid. He helped propagandize the society's claim that many lives could be saved if immediate action was taken after an accident. He used chiefly the powerful testimonials of those whose lives had already been saved. Today, we take this practice for granted.

Jealous competitors attacked Lettsom. They saw him as open game because he had become wealthy, spent freely, gave liberally, saw more patients than any of them, wrote numerous tracts, was easily charmed by a pretty girl (although completely faithful to his wife), and liked very much to be in the public eye. One satirist, a fellow doctor, penned the following cruel (and untrue) lines, which play on the fact that Latin uses "I" for "J."

When patients used to come to I,
  'Twas "I physics and I sweats 'em,"
When after that they chose to die,
    I did not grieve.
                                    —I. Lettsom

In generous deeds I gave my pelf,
  And though the world forgets 'em,
I never shall forget myself—
    What's due to Coakley Lettsom.

Although not overly strict in his Quaker observance, he always dressed as a Quaker and attended Quaker meetings. He put little stock in professions of faith unaccompanied by action. There is "only one true religion, consisting in doing unto others as we wish others should do to us." That this was his real belief and not a feigned one is perhaps best demonstrated by his encounter with a highwayman. The fellow pulled a gun on the doctor. Sensing that the man was not used to the trade, Lettsom questioned him, learned the tragic circumstances surrounding his fall into robbery, assisted him, and set him on an honest path.

To the end, he retained this faith, although he might have become bitter had he wished, for all his children died before him. "My path seems to be over the ashes of my children," he lamented. The most severe blow came when his eldest child died, for he had spent much time educating the boy in his own profession of medicine. Lettsom remarked that his boy had quitted the Society of Friends (Quakers) for that of angels.

10

Edward Jenner

(1749–1823)

The Man Who Conquered Smallpox

This is pure and undefiled religion in the sight of our
God and Father, to visit orphans and widows in their
distress, and to keep oneself unstained by the world.
(James 1:27 NASB*)*

Jenner stands for every doctor who took a lonely stand to fight an epidemic. Derided and persecuted, he has the distinction of being perhaps the only doctor ever to provide the world with the tools to eradicate a disease completely.

S mallpox was the terror and scourge of Europe. Thousands died each year of the dreaded disease. Others sought protection by being deliberately inoculated with the live smallpox virus. The technique had long been used in the Ottoman empire and was brought to England, where it was employed with perfect success by practitioners such as Thomas Dimsdale (who even inoculated Catherine the Great of Russia) but not so successfully by others. The hope was that those who were exposed to the virus would contract mild cases, but, of course, some people contracted severe cases, and a few were killed by the treatment. Even if the person who was inoculated did not contract the disease, anyone who came near him or her during the contagious period risked taking a serious infection. The practice was not at all satisfactory.

Edward Jenner was taken from his home to stables kept for the purpose of vaccination. Here he was bled and starved for the operation, given the treatment, and tied up to prevent his escape. He became very ill and declined. The once strong boy became sickly. For years, he heard noises. He was sent to a small school while he recovered, but he was so weak that his brother Stephen took him home. Their parents had died within weeks of each other when Edward was five, and Stephen had become his guardian.

The experience of vaccination may have imprinted young Jenner with terror. At any rate, it inclined him to be more than usually attentive to the clues that led him to develop the cowpox vaccine, a vaccine that eventually wiped out smallpox everywhere on earth, except in the laboratory.

After he recovered, Jenner was sent to study for the ministry. Although his father had been a clergyman, the boy took no interest in the pulpit. He wished to be a naturalist instead. Indeed, he collected many specimens and in due course taught himself the classification system of the famed Swedish naturalist Carl Linnaeus (1707–1778).

The lad's school days were unhappy. His schoolmaster caned him for asking questions and denounced him for buying scientific books. Scripture opposed science, he told Edward. Eventually, the abused boy fled home. After verifying Edward's story, Stephen allowed his ward to remain home, studying Latin, history, music, poetry, and his new, keen interest—medicine.

At thirteen, Jenner was apprenticed to surgeon John Ludlow. Although Jenner was still in weak health, he worked hard, assisting at surgeries. After his apprenticeship ended, Jenner moved to London, where he studied under the famous Dr. John Hunter. Hunter was a feisty man who cared little for convention. If something looked workable, he tried it.

Jenner doted on the bad-tempered man and his single-minded dictum: truth, truth, truth! Hunter, in turn, trusted Jenner and even left him in charge of his private practice when he went on his honeymoon. The youth lived for a time with the newlywed doctor and his bride, Anne, frequently reading to her while she sewed. In their house he met many outstanding people, including the poet-playwright Oliver Goldsmith, the painter Sir Joshua Reynolds, the explorer Captain Cook, and America's ambassador, Benjamin Franklin. He also met grave-diggers, whose unsavory trade was winked at by a government eager to provide better-trained anatomists for its warships. Hunter was infamous for paying "resurrectionists" to rob graves for bodies. Jenner learned anatomy by studying these stolen corpses.

Jenner turned his hand to other activities. He cataloged specimens for Captain Cook's botanist, Joseph Banks, completing in two months a job that most men could not complete in six. Impressed, Cook offered him a place on his ship, but Jenner declined. He was determined to become a surgeon. When Hunter offered him a partnership, the young man declined that, too. He wanted to return to the countryside.

Trade was slow in coming to the twenty-four-year-old Jenner when he returned as a doctor to Gloucestershire. Naturalism remained of interest to him and helped fill his empty hours. After he had made a careful study of the habits of the cuckoo, he attempted to publish his findings but met a good deal of opposition. The behavior he described seemed just too bizarre. Painstakingly he amassed more evidence and proved that cuckoos lay their eggs in other birds' nests and that fledgling cuckoos push out the other chicks when they hatch. The Royal Society was finally convinced and made him a member. Jenner also whiled away time playing the flute and writing poems. In 1788, he married.

Sometime during these years, Jenner learned from milkmaids that those who contracted cowpox were immune to smallpox. Hunter had heard the same story but had asserted that it was a myth. He had seen people contract smallpox after taking cowpox, he said. Jenner wondered if Hunter's exceptions might not be due to misdiagnosis. By careful research, he found that this was so. He continued his investigation for twenty years. Meanwhile, he implemented new ideas in his own treatment of smallpox. He stopped bleeding smallpox patients, giving their bodies a better chance to recover from the disease. He convinced many farmhands to accept a vaccination of cowpox, and none who did so caught smallpox.

Sure of his ground at last, Jenner put his idea to test, infecting a lad named Phipps with cowpox. Two months later, he inoculated the lad with live smallpox. A mob surrounded his house. If the boy died, Jenner would be hung as a murderer, swore the rioters. The boy proved immune. At last, Jenner had proof positive. Nonetheless, a pamphlet was printed denouncing him.

Neither was all well in the medical community. Doctors scorned Jenner and threatened him with expulsion from their fraternity. Medical journals refused even to print his account of his experiments.

Jenner was undeterred. Convinced by his first success, he worked selflessly to promote his idea. He could see that it was of such potential benefit to mankind that personal considerations must simply be set aside. As a result, he suffered financially, spending his own money on ceaseless investigations. He received little compensation, and because of medical attacks on his name, patients were reluctant to come to him. Jenner persisted in the teeth of this traditionalism.

In the end, of course, he was recognized with many honors. One by one, open-minded doctors read his book and conducted further tests. Today we think of him as the father of the science of virology and preventive medicine. He introduced the term *virus* to medical terminology. Even in his lifetime he became a revered figure.

How famous was he? During the Napoleonic wars, Bonaparte himself bowed to Jenner's name. The little Corsican honored an appeal to free a number of Englishmen held captive in France because it was made in Jenner's name.

Although other doctors had performed cowpox vaccinations before Jenner, they did so without any scientific certainty of its merits. Jenner was the first doctor to prove that infection with the mild disease definitely protected one against the more dangerous smallpox virus. He sought a systematic means of vaccinating the entire population and was the first to attempt to eliminate the dreaded disease from the entire world. He found a way to preserve cowpox virus alive so it could be transported overseas.

In gratitude for his work, Parliament voted him £10,000. With his usual selflessness, he used the money to assist needy doctors. The London College of Physicians, as stubborn as ever, refused him election because he would not allow them to test his knowledge of the antiquated theories of Galen and Hippocrates. Jenner could have agreed to their terms, but he thought that elimination of one of the world's most terrible and disfiguring scourges was sufficient qualification to make him a member of *any* medical society. He did without the honor.

Jenner's old age was lonely. His wife and eldest son died before him. Indeed, at the death of his first son, he suffered a breakdown. The loss of his wife was a great blow to him, for she was a gentle woman who brought him peace. She had conducted Scripture classes for neighbor children.

Jenner's character was also Christian. A friend wrote that the great man was always conscious of the presence of God. Jenner confirmed his religious views shortly before his death, saying, "I do not wonder that men are grateful to me, but I am surprised that they do not feel gratitude to God for thus making me a medium of good."

Jenner's was no easy life. In addition to his childhood sufferings, the premature loss of his wife and son, and his persecution by the medical establishment, he contracted typhus from a patient and nearly died. Another time, he almost froze to death while making a sick call. The day before his death, he walked to town to provide firewood for the poor at his own expense.

By his concern for the poor he demonstrated that he was a Christian. In his writing, he asked Christ to receive his imperishable soul. His name and work will be rememberd as long as the world remembers its benefactors.

11

James Derham

(BORN CA. 1762)

Doctor Despite Race Barriers

Therefore go and make disciples of all nations,
baptizing them in the name of the Father and of the
Son and of the Holy Spirit. (Matthew 28:19)

James Derham rose to eminence as a physician despite racial barriers. Much of his life was spent in slavery, yet he became the first professional African-American doctor in our country—at least, the first of whom we have any record. His achievement is all the more astonishing when one realizes that not for more than another century would it become commonplace for an African-American to achieve medical education in the United States. Derham stands for all doctors who overcame class barriers to give their services to fellow humans.

Ihave conversed with him upon most of the acute and epidemic diseases of the country where he lives, and was pleased to find him perfectly acquainted with the modern simple mode of practice in those diseases. I expected to have suggested some new medicines to him, but he suggested many more to me." With those words, Dr. Benjamin Rush (1746–1813) introduced James Derham to the world. Rush's testimony was no small tribute by a prominent citizen to a black man who had been a slave.

It is not easy to become a doctor at any time. But imagine the obstacles facing an African-American in the early years of the American republic. Even in the states that prohibited slavery, a man of African origin was viewed as an inferior simply because of his skin color. In Southern states, a black man was subject to slavery. Those who achieved emancipation could not rely on the security of their freedom. Cases of freed slaves being kidnapped were not unknown. Free blacks were barred from colleges and universities, and medical schools were no exception. In most cases, such rudimentary skills as reading and writing were kept from black people. To become a black physician was quite simply a matter of heroic achievement.

Black men who claimed to be doctors appeared early in America. Their skills probably did not advance much beyond bloodletting and the extraction of teeth, although they did use some herbal concoctions of real merit. Witch doctors persisted among slaves. Quacks preyed upon members of the downtrodden African race, who were often able to obtain little in the way of professional care if their owners were not disposed to employ a trained doctor for their relief.

James Derham is the first African-American from the United States known to have become a properly qualified physician. What little we do know about him is only because of his determination to obey a command of Christ. In 1788, Derham traveled from Catholic New Orleans (then under Spanish rule) to Philadelphia to be baptized in his childhood Episcopal faith. While in Philadelphia, James Derham met the physician and patriot, Benjamin Rush.

Rush was, at that time, the leading doctor of Philadelphia, perhaps even of the thirteen colonies. A graduate of Edinburgh, he was one of the best-trained physicians in the United States and actively engaged in the medical training of other doctors. His zeal for the American Revolution and for ratification of the Constitution made him prominent in the new-born United States. Furthermore, his energy had won him an international reputation and made him a member of several foreign societies. Therefore, his assessment of Derham is of some value. He presented information about Derham to the Pennsylvania Society for Promoting the Abolition of Slavery.

According to Rush, Derham was born a slave in Philadelphia around 1762. At some point early in his life, he learned to read and write. The boy was transferred to John Kearsley Jr. of Philadelphia, a physician and expert on throat diseases. Kearsley trained the boy to compound medicines and wait on patients.

The life of a slave was a life of uncertainty. John Kearsley was an ardent Tory; consequently, he opposed the American Revolution and sided with the British. Outraged patriots accused him of treason, carted him through the streets, and threw him into prison, where he became insane and died. Derham was sold. Passing through several hands, he became the property of Dr. George West, who was attached to a British regiment. He employed Derham in menial medical tasks. We can guess that the youth kept a sharp eye about him, picking up anatomical and surgical knowledge that would later make him an outstanding practitioner.

At the close of the Revolutionary War, West could not take Derham to Britain as property. Consequently, he sold the slave to yet a third doctor, Dr. Robert Dove of New Orleans, who made Derham his assistant. Derham proved so useful that Dove was moved to offer him his freedom upon easy terms. Two or three years later, Derham was free, and he set up practice under Dove's patronage. His education was in line with the medical education of the day. Of 3,500 doctors practicing in the United States around 1800, only four hundred could claim that they had attended medical school. The rest of them had learned their trade as apprentices to established doctors or by reading books.

It was perhaps providential that Derham wound up in New Orleans. Racial barriers were not so formidable in that French-Spanish city as in the United States. (Because the French did not possess

American prejudices against African-Americans, many African-Americans later traveled to France to attend medical school when U.S. colleges refused them admittance.) For Derham, French civility enabled him to practice his profession even among the white people of New Orleans. So great was his skill that he earned $3,000 a year, a very large sum for that day. We can put Derham's achievement into perspective by comparing his income with that of prominent contemporaries. Fifty years later, **John Story Kirkbride** thought he was doing well to earn $500 a year in Philadelphia. In 1804, the well-educated **Nathan Smith** was paid a mere $200 a year as founder and head professor of the Dartmouth College medical school.

Rush took an interest in Derham when the two met. In a communication to the Pennsylvania Abolition Society, he noted Derham's extraordinary abilities. The Philadelphia doctor went on to describe Derham as very modest and engaging in his manners. "He speaks French fluently and has some knowledge of the Spanish language." In his letter to the abolition society, Rush also noted the circumstances of Derham's baptism.

> By some accident, although born in a religious family belonging to the church of England, he was not baptized in his infancy, in consequence of which he applied a few days ago to Bishop White to be received by that ordinance into the Episcopal Church. The bishop found him qualified, both by knowledge and moral conduct, to be admitted to baptism, and this day performed the ceremony in one of the churches in this city.

That was November 14, 1788. For ten years after Derham returned to New Orleans, Rush and he corresponded, exchanging information. Rush sent copies of his own publications to the New Orleans doctor. We do not know when or under what circumstances Derham died. If any contemporary thought the fact worth recording, the record has been lost.

12

Nathan Smith

(1762–1829)

Educator of New England's Doctors

A faithful envoy brings healing. (Proverbs 13:17 NASB)

Nathan Smith was a selfless man who poured himself out for the medical welfare of New England. As an educator of doctors and the creator of educational institutions, he stands unrivaled in the annals of American medicine. Smith's importance is now obscured, but it was immense in his day. He stands for all doctors who selflessly serve others.

The young teacher listened attentively. Here was interesting news! Dr. Josiah Goodhue, the most notable physician in the region, was about to visit Putney, Vermont, to amputate a leg. "I'd like to see that," said Nathan Smith.

Several of the other fellows had the same idea. "Let's make up a party and go over," suggested someone. And so Nathan and his friends set out. A fellow never knew when the experience of amputating a leg might save a comrade's life—or his own.

As the men gathered, no one considered that it might distract the doctor or humiliate the patient to gawk at the operation. Goodhue himself did not seem to mind. "Could I have a couple volunteers?" he asked.

Anesthetics were as yet unknown. The unfortunate victim would have to be held down while the doctor operated. Smith stepped forward at once and was rewarded with the leg that was about to be removed. Other men took their places, and the doctor began his grisly job.

The school teacher's eyes did not miss a move as the doctor's swift knife sliced through tendons and his sharp saw sped through bone. His sensitive mouth tightened a few times in sympathy with the patient. An artery spurted. "Tie that off," commanded Goodhue. Using a bit of thread, Smith did. In about a minute, the leg was off.

Nathan felt a surge of elation. Surgery was not so mysterious after all. What he had just seen Goodhue do, he could do. After Dr. Goodhue had finished wiping up, Nathan approached him. "Will you train me?" he asked.

At that time in America, a man usually became a doctor by working with an established practitioner. For most men, no other course was possible. Only three medical schools existed in the United States, and those were of dismal quality by the standards of just fifty years later—standards Smith helped raise.

"What kind of education do you have?" asked Goodhue. "Any Latin? Any science?"

Nathan Smith recited his slight qualifications.

"Medicine is in a distressingly low state in these parts," said Goodhue reflectively. "I wish only properly qualified men to enter the field. Your education is lacking. Bring yourself up to the qualifications a man entering the general course at Harvard must possess and I'll see you get trained."

With that promise, Nathan had to content himself. But if Goodhue expected to hear no more from Smith, he did not know his man.

Nathan Smith was born September 30, 1762, in Massachusetts. His family soon moved to Vermont, where his father became a pioneer farmer. There Nathan was raised. Little is known of his childhood, except that he showed an early zeal for knowledge. He helped with farm work (as did all rural children in those days), fished, and hunted. On one of his hunting expeditions, his fellows left him with a small stock of food. Lost in a pine wilderness for three days, he came close to starving and freezing to death. To be lost was to risk capture by Indians. He did make it home, but near starvation and the consumption of improperly cooked food left him ill for several months.

Toward the end of the Revolutionary War, Nathan joined a militia to fight the Indians. On at least one occasion, he was ambushed and shot at by an Indian brave. Apparently, he distinguished himself; by the age of eighteen he had risen to the captaincy of his regiment. At nineteen, he became teacher of the district school. And then Dr. Goodhue visited Putney, Vermont.

Smith threw himself into intense study with Rev. Whiting of Rockingham, Vermont. Two years after the leg amputation, Smith knocked on Goodhue's door, ready to commence the promised training. Goodhue was as good as his word and agreed that Smith should assist him in return for board and tuition. Nathan Smith was then twenty-two. Three years later, he opened his own practice in Cornish, New Hampshire.

Two years of practice at Cornish showed Smith that, while his medical knowledge was far superior to the superstitions of the inhabitants, it was insufficient for the needs of his patients. Consequently, he set aside his practice for a time and traveled to Cambridge, Massachusetts, where he could study anatomy, surgery, *materia medica,* and the theory and practice of medicine. In 1790, he became only the seventh man to graduate with a Bachelor of Medicine from Harvard. His training was now superior to that of almost every American doctor.

Smith returned to Cornish and for three more years practiced medicine in that town and its surrounding environs. The next year he married. Two years later, he was a widower.

Perhaps the death of his wife made Nathan contemplate his own mortality. Time would not go on forever. And the demands upon his skill showed that more trained doctors were needed. He thought the matter through and in 1796 proposed to the New Hampshire legislature that a medical school be opened at Dartmouth. Meanwhile, he married Sarah Chase, half-sister of his late wife. The two of them had ten children, most of whom lived to maturity.

President Wheelock of Dartmouth favored Smith's plan. The trustees, however, while acknowledging its merit, determined to postpone a decision for at least a year. Smith was disappointed. However, since he intended to teach all the classes himself, he determined to put the time of waiting to good use and gain even more knowledge.

In the eighteenth century, the best medical school in the English-speaking world was at Edinburgh. Established by students of **Hermann Boerhaave**, the great Dutch doctor, and improved under the leadership of the Munro family, Edinburgh had begun a quiet revolution in the practice of medicine in Great Britain. So great was Nathan Smith's public spirit that he sailed to Scotland at his own expense to attend Edinburgh, leaving behind his wife and his first son, Solon, for a painful nine-month separation.

He had almost no funds; and the funds he did have were borrowed. But faith was evident in the words he wrote to Dr. Lyman Spalding at the onset of his voyage: "Respecting my voyage I am not so well provided for as I could wish, but must put my trust in God and not filthy lucre." In England, with his little money, he bought medical books and apparatus, expenditures he hoped Dartmouth would reimburse. He was homesick and yearned to return to Vermont. But he persevered, acquiring what he could of European practice before returning to the United States in 1797.

Smith's gamble paid off. Dartmouth's trustees agreed to allow him to proceed with his plan, although formal approval had to wait a year, until 1798. He would teach anatomy, surgery, chemistry, and physics. He must do so without a salary, they decreed. Students might pay him small sums if they chose.

To make a living, Smith would have to practice medicine on the side. This meant long horseback rides into the countryside. Patients often had scant means to pay him; income was small. So great was Smith's dedication to the cause of medical education, however, that he endured these unreasonable conditions and long periods of separation from his family, who remained in Cornish for the time being. As a further testimony of his civic concern, Smith bought most of the medical books for the school and even paid his assistant out of his own pocket! Not until 1804 did New Hampshire award him a salary: $200 a year.

Contention with the tight-fisted legislature, the ignorance of those who resisted allowing him to dissect bodies, weariness from overwork, and stomach problems came close to crushing this bold man's spirit. In 1810, Nathan Smith almost gave up. In retrospect, he appears to have suffered a nervous breakdown. He had to take time off to recover his health. But after he rebounded, he resumed his duties. In 1812, he was still attempting to collect $1,217 of his own money that he had spent on the school, a large sum for the day—money the legislature had promised to repay him. Still, he did not grow bitter. Always seeking the best for his students, he hired America's top anatomist to give a series of lectures at Dartmouth. It says much for Nathan Smith's character that many of his pupils became eminent doctors of post-Revolution America.

In 1813, Smith left Dartmouth for Yale. He had grown weary of the struggle with New Hampshire authorities. Yale's medical school was already functioning. It had, in fact, already graduated medical students, but Smith renovated and improved the medical program. He not only shared with his students his vast fund of medical knowledge but also petitioned for and received $20,000 from the Connecticut legislature to create new facilities. In gratitude, his will donated his valuable library of five hundred books to Yale.

These years were not without distress. Again Nathan Smith had to live apart from his family, this time for two years, until he could move them to New Haven. His beloved oldest daughter died, breathing joyful faith to the last, to be sure, but striking a deep blow to his heart all the same. Smith's own faith seems to have struggled with the free-thinking ideas of Paine, Voltaire, and other Deists about that time. At any rate, Timothy Dwight (1752–1817), who was president of the university and a man of deep Christian convictions, hesitated to call Smith to Yale on that score. In a letter to Dr. Mason Cogswell of Hartford, Smith wrote,

> Respecting Dr. Dwight's former objections to me, I freely acknowledge that they were well founded and such as a wise and good man would always consider as all important. My earnest prayer now is to live to undo all the evil I have done by expressing my doubts as to the truth of Divine Revelation, and to render to society all the good my talents and powers will permit me to do.

While still employed by Yale, Smith was consulted in the founding of the Medical School of Maine at Bowdoin College, and he gave expert testimony before the Maine legislature. Of his deep feelings for the value of medical education we can have no doubt. "A medical school does more toward ameliorating the condition of mankind than any other institution . . . ," he wrote to his former pupil and lifelong friend, Dr. Shattuck of Boston. To found a single medical school would be achievement enough for most men. Nathan Smith had already founded, or had a hand in founding, two schools and now was involved in founding a third. He would eventually have a hand in founding *five* such schools. When Bowdoin Medical School opened, he taught its first classes, a summer series.

Smith next helped his son Nathan Ryno Smith (1797–1877) establish Vermont's medical school. Again he was intimately associated with its founding, advising every aspect by letter and traveling to Burlington to present some of the first lectures.

With his fifth school, Nathan Smith was not so closely involved. Nathan Ryno Smith joined forces with Dr. George McClellan (1796–1847) to form the Jefferson Medical School of Philadelphia. Nathan Smith contributed articles and advice to the enterprise.

Smith's capacity for work was enormous. In addition to founding medical schools and teaching, he wrote a classic on typhoid (he called it typhous). He learned to reduce dislocations of the hip. Unaware that Ephraim McDowell (1771–1830) had performed an ovariotomy, he performed such an operation himself, believing he was breaking new ground. It was one of the first such operations performed in America. He also wrote on necrosis and issued a book on surgery.

Wherever the good doctor went, he was inundated by the sick. He often rode great distances, even into neighboring states, to treat patients. But in his sixties, even this energetic man began to slow down and had to cut his heavy work load.

In 1828, Smith suddenly suffered the symptoms of stroke. As it became apparent that he was approaching death, he took comfort in the Scriptures. During his life, he had attended church whenever occasion permitted. Now he consulted with several pastors and asked for their prayers.

He died poor materially. He had always given freely, both of his time and of his purse, to meet the needs of others.

Although Nathan Smith is little remembered today, such was not the case immediately following his death. At that time, notable men stepped forward to speak of the undying benefits of his lifework.

Woolsey, one of Yale's presidents, remembered how as a child he had adored Smith. "He was the most delightful, unselfish, and kind-hearted man I ever knew, and we children all loved him. He was confined to the house for a month by an injury to his leg, and it was a great treat for us to be in his room, and difficult to keep us out."

Friends remembered his wit. A young fellow named Lincoln came to his house asking for medicine. He returned again and again. One day Nathan Smith remarked, "I believe, Lincoln, you don't want any more medicine. It's my daughter you want." This proved to be the case. Lincoln became Smith's son-in-law.

A dull student once asked Smith if it would not be possible to transfer living, sentient brains from one head to another. Smith replied that ". . . if the gentleman who puts the question could make a discovery of this nature, it might prove of great advantage to himself."

Patients recalled his generosity and compassion. For instance, he wept when he had to take the leg off a terrified, trembling boy. Another time he rode some distance to take the leg off a man and asked a $50 fee. Bystanders generously raised the money because the man was destitute. As soon as the surgery was completed, Nathan Smith handed the $50 to the amputee and rode off.

Another acquaintance remembered his humility and delight in a practical joke. "One day he was riding through Guilford, a few miles east of New Haven, when a woman came out of the house and asked if he knew Dr. Smith, and if he were in New Haven, and explained that there was a case there requiring his attention. He inquired the particulars and said, 'I know Dr. Smith very well; he is not in New Haven, but I can attend the case just as well as he can.' He did so, performing the necessary operation, and rode away without telling anyone who he was."

Students remembered his cheerfulness, clearheadedness, and hard work. His memory was so well developed that he was able to lecture on complex subjects without notes.

Selfless men should be remembered. New England owes the education of her doctors to the selflessness of Nathan Smith.

13

Sir Charles Bell

(1774–1842)

Anatomist of the Nerves

Blessed are the pure in heart, for they will see God.
(Matthew 5:8)

It is given to some doctors to make breakthroughs that have eluded earlier generations. Charles Bell's genius was focused upon the nervous system, on which he shed a new light of understanding. Except for the work of Haller, few significant developments had occurred for fourteen hundred years. Bell exemplifies the type of researcher who changed our knowledge of the human body at the time when the microscope was brought into everyday use and human dissection became standard practice.

In December 1807, Charles Bell wrote an excited letter to his older brother, George. George Bell had long been supportive of Charles, and the two corresponded regularly. This closeness had existed from childhood and was later augmented by the boys' marriages to the Shaw sisters, Barbara and Marion. Charles needed George, for despite being a brilliant surgeon and researcher, he was somewhat prone to hesitation, self-doubt, and depression. In some respects, his older brother had taken the place of a father for him, for Rev. William Bell had died when Charles was but five. The December letter to George flamed with a sense of great discovery.

"My new *Anatomy of the Brain* is a thing that occupies my head almost entirely," he wrote. "I hinted to you formerly that I was burning, or on the eve of a grand discovery. . . ." After describing to his brother the seats in the brain to which he had traced specific nerves, Charles Bell added, "My object is not to publish this, but to lecture it—to lecture to my friends—to lecture to Sir Jos. Banks' coterie, to make the town ring with it, as it is the only new thing that has appeared in anatomy since the days of Hunter; and, if I make it out, as interesting as the circulation or the doctrine of absorption. But I must still have time."

He needed time for two reasons. With his habitual self-distrust, he doubted his own findings, and he needed to make more experiments to clarify certain points. But those were experiments he hated to make. In the days before anesthetic, animals had to be cut open while they were fully conscious, and they suffered terrible pain. This practice greatly troubled Charles, and he preferred to put it off as long as possible. So, although he lectured, he did not publish until 1811. Ten years later, he sent his assistant, Alexander Shaw, to France, where Shaw demonstrated Bell's latest discoveries to Magendie and others. Within a year, Magendie had advanced and simplified Bell's views so much that their findings are today called the Bell-Magendie Law.

If the average citizen has heard of Charles Bell at all, it is most likely in connection with a medical condition he described: Bell's Palsy. He showed that care must be taken not to cut the facial nerve that controlled the affected muscle. But although he is largely forgotten now, Charles might honestly, without bragging, have crowed a good deal louder to George. Although **Albrecht von Haller** had recently done good work on the nerves and muscles, Bell's findings were a leap forward in the anatomy and function of the nervous system and followed fourteen hundred years of negligible advance.

His interest in the nervous system began when he was but a student. An older brother, John, was a brilliant anatomist who lectured and published. Barely into his teens, Charles assisted John and before he reached manhood became a capable surgeon skilled in comparative anatomy. At fourteen, he entered the university; by his early twenties, he had contributed an article on the nervous system—illustrated with his own drawings—to John's anatomy text; at twenty-four, he published *A System of Dissection* with plates engraved from his own drawings; and at twenty-five, he was admitted to the College of Surgeons.

Faith played its part in focusing his mind. Charles's father and grandfather had been ministers. His mother was a minister's daughter and possessed a sweet and self-sacrificing disposition. At the University of Edinburgh, Charles came under the teaching of Dugald Stewart, a philosopher of deep spiritual conviction, whose teaching affected Charles with a sense of eternal values. As we shall see, these values surfaced again and again throughout his life.

The University of Edinburgh had no position for Charles Bell once he graduated. Brilliant men already held the few available professorships. In the days before anesthetic, surgeons made their name by speed. A surgeon who could take off a leg in under a minute was greatly prized. Charles was good but not of that caliber. He decided to move to London, a rapidly growing metropolis, where he hoped for wider opportunity. At the age of thirty, he made the move.

London, alas, offered few immediate prospects. His income did not suffice for his needs. George, a successful businessman, had to relieve his brother's finances. With little professional work to do, Charles produced a book. A talented artist, he analyzed works of Western art in relation to what he had learned of anatomy, writing and illustrating his *Essay on the Anatomy of Expression in Painting.* This book established his name internationally. As in his earlier work, art and anatomy fused together.

Gradually, Charles created a place for himself as teacher and surgeon in London. He built up a wonderful museum of samples, among which were wax models he made of interesting cases. He was fortunate to acquire the former school of John Hunter, the famed surgeon who had trained a generation of British doctors, including **Edward Jenner**. Charles continued to study the nervous system.

Charles's studies nearly did not see the light of day. In 1809, John Shaw, one of his house pupils and soon to be his brother-in-law, took scarlet fever and nearly died. Charles nursed him. In the process, he contracted the dangerous disease himself, and John Shaw, in turn, kept him alive. John, like all of Charles's students, revered him for his gentleness. When he had recovered sufficiently to do so, Charles continued his study of the nervous system, discovering the difference between sensory and motor nerves, a breakthrough of enormous magnitude. He published his first results in 1811 and continued to correct them afterwards. That same year, he married Marion Shaw, John's sister.

His publications made his name, and he won election to the Middlesex Hospital staff of surgeons. The hospital prospered under its association with him. His house school became the hospital's medical school. Curiously enough, although Charles hated to see suffering in either man or animal, he apparently felt no qualms about paying grave robbers for bodies to dissect. In this respect, he was like all of the other surgeons of his day.

As slow as Charles might have been to publish his findings and as hesitant as he was to cut live animals unnecessarily, he was swift to respond to need. One night as he was walking home through the streets, he heard a woman scream for help. Her husband had cut his throat. He rushed up and saved the man's life by applying pressure along the wound until surgeons arrived with tools to sew it up. Those were the years of Napoleon's brutalization of Europe. When English soldiers returned wounded from the wars, Charles volunteered his services, attending them until he was beyond exhaustion from overwork and weeping. On the day that news reached England of the victory at Waterloo, Charles grabbed his surgical bag, and, without passport, sailed across the channel, rushing to the front where he might salvage the wounded. Many injured soldiers had lain for days without medical attention by the time he arrived. The stench was nauseating. For a week, he worked twenty-three hours a day on ghastly, infected wounds, saving first as many Englishmen as he could and then turning his attention to the French.

War between France and Britain did not prevent Charles from sharing his findings with French researchers. In 1821, he sent John Shaw to demonstrate their latest discoveries to Francois Magendie (1783–1835), sharing with him all their work, both published and unpublished. International rivalry may have contributed to Charles's crying "foul" when the following year Magendie published a brilliant essay that clarified points on which Charles had been vague. There is little doubt that Magendie built on Charles's work and quickly surpassed it. Heated words were exchanged in which Charles did not shine at his best.

In 1825, Charles moved back to Edinburgh to accept a professorship, relinquishing all that he had so painstakingly established in London. The move was a mistake. His new professorship did not pay enough to support him. He was unable to compete as a surgeon because brilliant young men such as James Syme (1799–1870)— who became **Joseph Lister's** father-in-law—had a lock on the field. To pay his bills, he had to drive himself beyond his physical ability. His health declined. He developed heart trouble.

In these dark days, however, he did not lose faith. The Earl of Bridgewater left a will requesting that treatises be written to "illustrate the power, wisdom and goodness of God, as manifested in Creation." Charles was asked to contribute, and he chose as his theme: "The Hand; its mechanism and vital endowments, as evincing design, and illustrating the power, wisdom and goodness of God."

In the treatise, he took mankind to task for thanklessness. He noted that we take for granted many of God's gifts to us which we do not even recognize until they are snatched from us. The design of the hand is but one example. The leverage built into it, the beauty of design by which all fingers, despite their unequal length, meet equally on the palm, the opposition of the thumb with strength equal to that of the fingers, the brilliant variety and specialization of animal hands—all to Bell were evidences of design. As a Christian, he knew that Christ was the creator of this marvel.

Wednesday evening, April 27, 1842, Charles and Marion Bell read a passage of Scripture and sang a hymn together as they did every morning and evening. It so happened that the Scripture chosen for the day was Psalm 23, and no passage could have been more fitting: *Yea, though I walk through the valley of the shadow of death, I will fear no evil.* Charles was in pain that night, but it passed.

The next morning, he woke again in pain. He died suddenly and quietly, his head on Marion's shoulder. A great man, he did much in his quiet way to extend our knowledge of the working of the body and to prevent unnecessary and destructive surgery. He passed into eternity, there to meet his Lord—who had designed not only the hand but also the nervous system, of which Charles Bell was ever an astute student and anatomist. His gravestone has a simple inscription, drawn from the words of Christ: "Blessed are the pure in heart, for they shall see God."

14

René Théophile Hyacinthe Laënnec

(1781–1826)

Inventor of the Stethoscope

*I made a covenant with my eyes not to look lustfully
at a girl. (Job 31:1)*

Many medical tools are as old as the profession. Who
invented the first forceps? Who designed the lancet?
These questions may be unanswerable. Other tools
have come into use more recently. Paré invented the
surgical truss. Simpson introduced the sponge tent.
Lister designed a hook to remove small objects from
an ear. The stethoscope is so much the symbol of medicine that it comes as a shock to remember that it has
been with us less than three centuries. It was the invention of René Laënnec, who thus becomes an example
of the doctor as inventor.

When René Laënnec's mother died, his dilettante father, Théophile, rid himself of two sons and a daughter by farming them out to relatives. Laënnec was then but five years old. When he was seven, it was his good fortune to be shuffled off to live with his uncle Guillaume, a doctor and professor at Nantes, who inculcated in his young charge an interest in the medical profession. Out of that interest and the modesty of one of Laënnec's female patients came the stethoscope and greater understanding of internal diseases.

Those were the terrible days of the French Revolution. A peasant army entered Nantes. After fierce fighting that left many dead and wounded, they withdrew. Doctor Guillaume tended the injured while René prepared the bandages.

Guillaume sided with the Jacobins. However, he boldly opposed their cruel excesses, thereby bringing himself into grave danger. The revolutionary government of Paris dispatched a brute named Carrier to Nantes. Already men and women had been guillotined within sight of Uncle Guillaume's house at Nantes. Carrier stripped others naked and then either tied them together and drowned them or herded them onto barges, which were then sunk. The banks of the Loire were littered with corpses. Other victims of this sadist were mowed down by chain shot in nearby fields.

Laënnec's young eyes could not be entirely shielded from these atrocities. In spite of the turmoil, he persisted in his studies, for his instructors stoically held classes as though nothing unusual were happening. It was hard for the boy to keep up the pretense, however, when Uncle Guillaume was arrested.

Guillaume was fortunate. His bold words cost him only six weeks of detention at the hospital. He was released unharmed and later testified against Carrier when his brutalities became too gross for even the thugs in Paris to stomach. After that, Laënnec no longer needed to fear that his beloved uncle would be killed as so many others had been.

Over his father's opposition, René decided to study medicine. "[A] profession for fools," snorted his stepmother. But Guillaume obtained a low-ranking position for him in a dreary hospital, and this brought René a little money. During the revolution, the young man worked in city hospitals and even ventured into the ranks of the Republican army, practicing for his profession on the all-too-plentiful wounded and sick. For years, he studied hard and practiced medicine fitfully, unable to obtain parental consent to pursue it as a career.

But medicine did not consume all of his hours. Despite suffering "asthma"—probably the first symptoms of tuberculosis—he learned to play the flute. Like his father, he dabbled in poetry. A self-portrait made a couple of years before his death shows that he became a competent sketcher. At every opportunity, he tramped the country-side, fascinated with botany. He returned from these expeditions bloody-nosed and ill. He learned Greek and Latin so he could read medical classics in their original tongues, and the Breton language so he could draw closer to his roots. Uncle Guillaume pleaded with Théophile to authorize René to study medicine in Paris.

Finally, Théophile relented in his opposition. Immediately, René tramped the two hundred miles to Paris. He arrived sick and feverish but threw himself into his medical studies. In the following years, despite continual illness, he accomplished great things.

He won prizes in medicine and surgery. To supplement his mea-ger income, he gave anatomy lessons. A close observer, Laënnec was the first to give an accurate description of peritonitis, adhesions, false membranes, and other intestinal features. He was the first to give a reasonably accurate account of the function of the prostate. Medical journals accepted his papers. Paying positions eluded him, however, and continued to do so for many years. One of his original discoveries was that tubercular lesions can form in parts of the body besides the lung. This fact was far from obvious. (Ironically, it was of tuberculosis that he died, although he refused to the very end to admit that he suffered it. His mother and four siblings died of the same disease.)

When Laënnec completed his thesis, Théophile urged him to dedi-cate it to some high government official who might notice him and give him a hand up. Laënnec shrugged off the advice. With his char-acteristic fidelity, he dedicated the thesis to Guillaume instead. Gradu-ally, he rose in eminence, gaining patients, assuming an editorship, and cofounding a medical society. Students from Breton, new to

Paris, turned to him as their natural guide because he understood their dialect.

On March 17, 1803, Laënnec took a step that was much questioned and ridiculed—he embraced Catholicism. Laënnec's Catholicism was a deliberate choice made in his twenties. Reared without faith by his uncle, who despised the clergy, he came to the church consciously. "I have turned toward Him who alone can give me real happiness," he wrote his father. After that, whenever he visited Breton, he joined the procession of peasants who made their way to church every Sunday, and he shared their faith in the God of their fathers. Once he expressed the hope that someday he would have as much faith as the average Breton peasant woman. René never wavered from this spiritual commitment, no matter how the fortunes of the church increased or waned as governments rose and fell.

By Laënnec's day, physicians had learned to auscultate by applying their ears directly to the human chest to listen to what was going on inside the body. One young girl who came to Laënnec was stout-chested and felt some embarrassment at such an intimacy. Many a hard-boiled doctor would simply have scoffed and pushed ahead with the procedure; a weak man might have skipped the examination altogether. Laënnec, however, was of at once a gentler and a sterner cast. The girl probably had heart problems. He wanted to show consideration for her feelings, but she needed to be examined. He had to find a way to proceed.

Physics had taught him something about the transmission of sound. In a moment of inspiration, it occurred to him that he might roll up a tube of paper tightly and apply it to the girl's chest. When he tried this expedient, he was startled to discover how much more clearly he could hear the sounds within her than he had heard those in other patients. In that moment, the stethoscope was born.

Immediately, Laënnec sought to improve his invention. Discarding a number of unworkable solutions, he hit upon the idea of whittling wooden pieces that could be disassembled easily. With characteristic simplicity, he carried his new instrument inside his hat so he would have it with him whenever he needed it! He saw at once the good the stethoscope could do. Doctors cannot treat what they cannot diagnose. The stethoscope allowed René to make a whole new range of observations. From that day, he attempted to correlate chest and abdominal sounds with specific anatomical functions.

Gradually, Laënnec classified all of the cardiac and pulmonary sounds he heard, explaining their significance. Among the diseases he described were gangrene of the lungs, pneumonia in all stages, tuberculosis (consumption), emphysema, and bronchitis. To ensure that his fellow doctors employed the new diagnostic tool, he carved and handed out extra stethoscopes. Just as importantly, he printed descriptions based on his research.

In 1819, Laënnec was forced to discontinue practice and return to the countryside to regain his health. Clearly, he had tuberculosis. When he returned to Paris, he received a high appointment from the Royalist government, which had supplanted the revolutionaries. His writings drew attention and set a new fashion—they were actually clear and readable. Doctors came from all over the world to study his methods. They could not help being impressed by his gentle speech and anatomical skill. They could hear for themselves the value of the stethoscope once he had taught them the sounds for which they should listen.

Like his famous predecessor **Hermann Boerhaave**, he conducted class in Latin so that students of all the European nationalities could understand him. His method was to take a patient's history, examine the patient, allow trainees to examine the patient, discuss their findings, prescribe a treatment, and, if the patient died, conduct an autopsy. This method became widely imitated.

But the ointment of his success was not without flies. He became the focus of jealous attacks. Although he responded clearly and with good humor, these assaults on his name hurt him deeply. One campaign of calumny led him to marriage. To ease his household burdens, Laënnec took a housekeeper, a pious, middle-aged Catholic woman of high repute. Neighbors wagged their tongues. His enemies accused him of immorality. To quiet them and to restore her good name, he married her and found himself happy. His happiness lasted barely two years. By 1826, he was too ill to continue work and retreated again to the country. He died six weeks after his return to Breton, removing his rings from his fingers shortly before death (he explained) to spare anyone else the unpleasant task. He bade farewell to this world little richer than when he entered it.

Laënnec gave the world a brilliant new tool for diagnosis, and his practical observations demonstrated how the new tool might be used. With his invention dawned a new era in physical diagnosis.

15

Sir John Richardson

(1787–1865)

Navy Surgeon and Administrator

*May the Lord direct your hearts into God's Love and
Christ's perseverance. (2 Thessalonians 3:5)*

To single out *navy surgeon* and *administrator* as titles
for Sir John Richardson is to do him injustice. Yes, Sir
John was a navy surgeon and a forward-looking medical administrator, but he also was a loyal friend, a sailor,
a naturalist, an author, and a philologist. As explorer, he
ventured several times into arctic regions where no
European had gone before. As naturalist, he opened the
field of arctic biology. Enough animals and plants were
named after him to supply a small zoo. He wrote many
articles and books, including a four-volume work on the
fauna of the Arctic. When his friend John Franklin disappeared, he risked his life and sacrificed his savings to
locate him. In retirement, he was a volunteer reader on
a dictionary project. All doctors make life-and-death
decisions. Richardson was forced to make such a decision in a bold and open manner. Hundreds of medical
men have been public servants, but Richardson represents the best of that tradition.

S ir John Richardson died as he lived—active and in the Word of God. Monday, June 5, 1865, was a lovely day, perfect for overseeing the gardeners and driving his wife to visit friends. That evening, he sat with pen and paper, culling words from Wycliffe's translation of Isaiah and noting their use in context. He was committed to reading several early-English books for the creation of a new dictionary that would show how the words had been used. (This evolved into the *Oxford English Dictionary.*) He especially enjoyed working with the Wycliffe, he said, because it gave him profit as well as pleasure.

At 10 P.M., he led family worship, reading a passage from Matthew's gospel. Afterwards, he stood at the window and admired a fine moon. It would be full in two days, he noted, and he planned to drive to Ambleside. He kissed his daughter good night and went to bed, carrying with him an Anglo-Saxon translation by Alfred the Great. A few minutes later, Lady Richardson came up. As he was speaking with her about the morrow's plans, he gasped once quite suddenly and died. He was probably struck down by an embolism or coronary blockage.

Nation, friends, and family were surprised. Although John outlived all but one of his eleven brothers and sisters, he had been in the full vigor of life. With his passing, they realized that a great man was gone. His contributions had elevated every sphere he entered.

Richardson was born in 1787 in Dumfries, Scotland. As a boy, he farmed, swam, fished, climbed rocks, and walked the neighboring hills.

Exercise developed his body, but Richardson's mind developed also. At four, he learned to read. Children's books had not yet come into vogue, so he read adult works and demonstrated a tremendous capacity for retention. He memorized Bible passages and the poems of the Scottish bard Robert Burns.

In fact, Robert Burns was Richardson's neighbor in Dumfries for five years. On Sunday evenings, the great poet visited the Richardson home and more than once listened to little John recite the Psalms and corrected his errors. In this manner, Richardson was reared.

In 1800, the lad was apprenticed to a surgeon, his uncle, Dr. James

Mundell. He was a mere thirteen, but boys were expected to be useful at a much younger age in those days. There were three ways of becoming a doctor: apprenticeship, license, and university education. Richardson's apprenticeship would have sufficed to make him a medical practitioner; many doctors had no better credentials than that. Richardson, however, wanted more. At fourteen, he obtained permission to attend the University of Edinburgh. For the rest of his apprenticeship, he alternated his residence between Edinburgh and Dumfries.

Upon his uncle's death, he served under Samuel Shortridge. During those years at Edinburgh, Richardson brushed elbows with the novelist Walter Scott, the scientists Rutherford and Black, the artist Raeburn, and the moral philosopher Dugald Stewart. In 1807, Richardson was licensed by the Royal College of Surgeons in Edinburgh. He now had acquired the right to practice medicine through two of the paths open to him. In time, he would also complete his degree, making him one of the best-trained doctors of the day.

From 1804 through 1806, Richardson gained practical experience as house surgeon to the Galloway and Dumfries infirmary, a nursing home for the elderly. He lived simply and in his spare time continued healthful activities, roaming along beaches and up the Firth of Forth. He climbed nearby hills and crags.

When the navy appointed him assistant surgeon on the frigate *H.M.S. Nymphe,* he was as physically fit as any man aboard. Those were war years, and he participated in action on the Baltic Sea near Denmark, in Portugal, and in the United States. After a raid into Portugal, he was commended by his captain as cool and brave under fire.

His advancement was swift. By May 1808, he was acting surgeon of *H.M.S. Hercule,* a promotion awarded for "gallant conduct" and "devotion to duty." But trouble lay ahead.

Richardson's next ship was the *Blossom.* Captain Henry Probyn was a suspicious man who did not get on well with his subordinates. Manipulated by a scheming purser, Probyn came to believe that his officers were planning mutiny. He clapped two of them in irons.

Finally, Richardson, too, was arrested "on suspicion of his having been privy and concealing mutinous expressions." To spare them anxiety, Richardson reported the matter to his family only after his hearing. "I was tried yesterday by court-martial, when the charges were so ridiculous, and my conduct proved to be so correct, that I was honorably acquitted without even the trouble of making a defense." Probyn was removed from command and never given another ship.

An appointment as surgeon to the marines brought Richardson to America, where he witnessed the sack of Washington, D.C., and was appalled when the British burned the public library, an action he termed "barbaric." All of his life, he delighted in books. He mentioned often in his letters home whatever library he and his fellow officers were able to put together on his various ships. He himself sailed with as many as a hundred books at a time.

Placed on half pay after 1815 because of the cessation of hostilities, Richardson returned to Edinburgh to complete his studies. He wrote his thesis on yellow fever but contributed nothing new to the understanding of the dread disease. Eager for new opportunities, he took classes in natural history, hoping that he might win an appointment to some voyage of discovery, now that the Napoleonic and American wars were over. He married. And he applied to accompany John Franklin's expedition to explore the Arctic and search for a Northwest Passage. He was accepted. Franklin and he became fast friends, Richardson describing Franklin as "steady, religious, and cheerful." He could also have been describing himself.

The arctic journey proved profitable for geography and naturalism, but terrible for the men. Richardson had brought with him several pieces of scientific equipment, such as geological hammers and a portable microscope that he put to use. He made copious notes on the wildlife as the expedition traced the path of the Coppermine River to its mouth for the first time and charted many miles of Canada's northern coast.

Hunger and disease, however, took many lives. Richardson learned the meaning of solitude. "How dreadful if without faith in God!" he wrote. That faith would be tested again and again. The party was reduced to eating lichens and shoe leather. One of Richardson's companions, Robert Hood, became so ill from cold and starvation that he was slowing everyone down. Richardson urged the others to go forward under Franklin while he remained behind with the suffering man. A Christian seaman, John Hepburn, insisted on remaining with Richardson. To keep warm, the three huddled under blankets in their tent. They read Christian books they had toted along despite their waning strength. Morning and night they held religious services and found encouragement in their faith.

One day, Michel, one of the party, appeared with a note from Franklin, which he presented to Richardson. Franklin said that Jean Baptiste Belanger was being sent back with Michel because he could not keep pace with the others. Belanger did not appear. Michel claimed that the man had vanished—probably lost his way, he said. The men had to accept his story. Michel brought desperately needed meat. He had shot a hare and a partridge. On the strength of that meat, Richardson, Michel, Hepburn, and Hood were able to move forward. Hood's progress was slow, endangering them all. Richardson had to support him with an arm most of the time.

While Richardson and Hepburn were gathering lichens to eat, Michel shot Hood through the back of the head. He claimed it was an accident. The other two made no accusations, and the companions traveled warily on. Michel became increasingly defiant toward Richardson and openly threatened Hepburn. Although no one had accused him of wrongdoing, he ranted and protested his innocence. The two sailors suspected that Michel had killed Belanger. Now his ranting led them to believe that he had eaten his victim and two other men who had vanished earlier in the expedition. They remembered with a shudder the time that Michel had brought flesh into the camp, claiming it was part of a wolf "killed by a deer."

Michel left camp to gather lichens. Hepburn and Richardson discussed the situation. They decided that Michel must die. Dual roles warred in Richardson. As a doctor, he was dedicated to saving life. As a commander, he must enforce obedience and justice. Michel was stronger than both of them together and heavily armed. It would be a dangerous bit of work. Hepburn offered to do it, but Richardson refused. As commander, the responsibility fell to him. When Michel returned, Richardson faced and shot him.

Although his action was justifiable as self-defense and a commander's need to quell mutiny, and although Michel had murdered Hood and probably three other men, including Belanger, Richardson ever rued the execution as a "dreadful act." He never boasted of it. He said that if it had been just himself and Michel he would not have done it, but he thought that he had an obligation to protect Hepburn. After that unhappy incident, Hepburn and Richardson struggled forward and reached Franklin at Fort Enterprise.

Franklin was so ill that Richardson had to take charge. Despite his own weakness, he imposed his stern will upon the men, compelling them to clean up the fort, and he instituted daily religious services. The two leaders encouraged one another with the biblical promise, "Wait on the Lord. Be of good courage and he shall strengthen thine heart."

Their faith was vindicated. Franklin had promised one of the Indian tribes a shipment of goods to be delivered at a later date if the Indians would bring meat now. The Indians arrived with meat in November. The starving men fell upon the food like ravenous wolves. A week later, the survivors were fit for travel and reached Fort Providence. They had journeyed more than 5,500 miles in the Americas. Only nine of the twenty men who set out in good health returned alive.

When he reached England, Richardson issued a four-volume set on the fauna of Arctic America. Superbly illustrated, the volumes on quadrupeds and fish were completely his own work, and the volumes on insects and birds he prepared with collaborators. He was elected a fellow of the Royal Society.

The navy appointed him chief medical officer of the Melville Naval Hospital. Quickly and conscientiously, he reorganized the hospital to be more efficient. Shortly after he took the position at Melville, Richardson's wife died. Within a couple of years, he married one of Franklin's nieces. She bore him seven children.

Ten years after his appointment to Melville, the navy put

Richardson in charge of the Royal Hospital Haslar. Hasler carried a heavy patient load. James Lind (1716–1794) had made it a center for clinical research, especially on the problem of scurvy, which was so detrimental to sailors. But the institution also had its problems, and Richardson sought to reform it. To end patient neglect, he required doctors to visit their patients first thing in the morning, even before breakfast, and he set the example by his own actions. Over the opposition of naval traditionalists, he insisted on introducing anesthetics to relieve the torments of surgery.

Yellow fever, typhus, malaria, scurvy, tuberculosis, cholera, smallpox, and venereal disease were among the deadly afflictions he battled. During epidemics, he worked night and day. Cures existed for none of these scourges, although remedies such as quinine and citrus juice were useful for malaria and scurvy, respectively. Richardson's common sense led him to advocate cleanliness, fresh air, and space between patients as helpful to their recovery and the prevention of the spread of infection.

Richardson also reformed the treatment of mentally disturbed sailors. Until his administration, they had been treated as criminals. He insisted that they no longer be chained but rather allowed a certain amount of freedom and provided with occupational therapy and entertainment. He even allowed his own children to participate in outings with the mentally ill.

To bring the nursing staff under military discipline, he dismissed the civilian nurses, who were at any rate untrained, and drew his nurses from among the sailors. Later, he employed nurses from a specially created military corps of professional nurses. Florence Nightingale (1820–1910) and he had a long talk during which they found that their ideas coincided.

Always one to value a book, Richardson built the Hasler collection into a top-notch science library. Geologist Charles Lyell and naturalist Charles Darwin were two famous men who received permission to research at Richardson's superb library. Prevented by his duties from further field work, Richardson used his contacts to obtain specimens of fish from all over the world. He became a leading ichthyologist.

In 1840, Richardson's influence grew. He was made Inspector of Hospitals. He used this bully pulpit to trumpet medical reforms. Reforms were slow in coming, however, because top brass did not want change. Richardson was passed over for promotion to Director General of the Naval Medical Service because he ruffled too many feathers.

In 1845, Franklin sailed on another voyage to explore the last three hundred miles of the Northwest Passage, but Richardson was unable to join the expedition. His second wife died that year, leaving him with five small children to tend. Devoted to wife and family, Richardson took the blow hard. His home life had been happy. "It is only necessary to see the invariable cheerfulness and goodness of Sir John Richardson in his own house, and his attention to those most dependent on his kindness to form a true value of his admirable character," wrote an acquaintance who spent much time with the family. Another friend described him as "gentle as a woman." When a niece died, he wrote tenderly to his sister to comfort her, reminding her that "our Redeemer" had said "allow the little children to come to me." Richardson soon remarried for the sake of his children.

It was as well that Richardson did not accompany Franklin, for Franklin disappeared. So concerned was Richardson for the safety of his friend that he offered to lead a search for him. Richardson was then near sixty, but he retained an almost youthful vigor. Although his retirement was not well provided for, he cashed in his £500 life insurance policy to help equip the expedition to search for Franklin. He and Dr. John Rae were appointed commanders.

Again Richardson experienced the rigors of Canada's arctic winter. This time, however, he was better prepared and did not go hungry. Richardson and Rae split up to cover different territory. Richardson was often alone with French Canadians, with whom he could not share much conversation. "It is a great consolation to me, at such times, to offer up petitions for you and the children and for all my friends and connections. I do not forget to pray for my enemies, although I am not conscious I have one," he wrote home.

When weather forced him to remain in shelter for many weeks, he read the Bible, the prayer book, and Shakespeare, and had daily devotions.

Richardson did not find Franklin. One day, he suffered a fainting spell while walking. Realizing that he could no longer trust his body to carry him as it had when he was young, he returned home, leaving the younger Rae to pursue the search. In England, he resumed his duties and kept up a charity practice among the poor. He wrote and developed his interest in comparative linguistics and the origins of words. To the end he exercised regularly, considering it no hardship to follow twenty miles of Hadrian's wall when he was seventy-five. Because of this, friends and relatives were surprised by his sudden death.

The body dies, but the spirit lives on. At the end of his full-length biography of Richardson, Robert E. Johnson wrote, "To a critical twentieth-century biographer, there is almost a duty, if possible, to 'debunk' a Victorian great, but the present biographer has uncovered nothing in the public or private life of Sir John Richardson that would diminish his mental, moral, religious, or physical stature." Another admirer wrote, "I never saw a mind more finely balanced than Sir John's. . . . He has the kindest, gentlest heart, and the most sweet and gentle temper, with a fund of information." Such was the character of this doctor who followed Christ.

16

Thomas Hodgkin

(1798–1866)

Discoverer of Hodgkin's Disease

*Do not forsake your friend and the friend of your
father. (Proverbs 27:10)*

Doctors who are the first to describe a disease or to
make original observations of its nature or cure are often rewarded by having the disease named for them.
Thomas Hodgkin was the first person to describe a
number of cases of a rare lymphatic disorder. It is now
known as Hodgkin's Disease. He stands for all those
doctors who have had a disease named for them.

B ecause the man was so very ill, Thomas Hodgkin sat up all night with him. The man recovered. In gratitude, he handed Hodgkin a blank check and told him to fill it out for any amount he liked. Thomas wrote it out for ten pounds.

"Why did you make it out for so little?" asked the astonished patient.

"Thou dost not look as if thou could'st afford more," replied Hodgkin.

As it turned out, the patient was very wealthy. He was so offended by Hodgkin's unintentional slight that he never employed him again.

The incident was characteristic of Hodgkin. A lifelong Quaker, there was never a more unworldly doctor. Money, fame, position, fashion—none of these things swayed him. When he had money, he shared it with the poor. Shy, he did not crow about himself or his accomplishments; therefore, he never became famous. When he was repeatedly passed over for the post of Assistant Physician at Guy's Hospital, where he had done his best work, he was dejected but did not complain. As for his dress, all of his life he wore the dark, plain clothes of a Quaker.

During his lifetime, he won little recognition. Not until thirty years after his death were his merits recognized. Even then, some dispute existed as to whether he deserved credit for the disease named for him since his pupil, Dr. Samuel Welles, added his own observations to Hodgkin's original description and made this deadly disease of the lymphatic system better known.

And yet Hodgkin is a doctor worth remembering. He was one of the three men who made Guy's Hospital, London, a great teaching center of early nineteenth-century England, a time when clinical medicine began to flourish.

Hodgkin was born in London. His father was a tutor to fashionable young ladies, teaching, among other things, grammar and exquisite penmanship. John Hodgkin was a man who had undergone exciting and varied experiences. Perhaps Hodgkin's shyness was owing to a perceived inability to compete with his versatile father. John gave Thomas his early lessons. John must have been a good teacher, for all of his sons made names for themselves. Probably it was from his father that Thomas Hodgkin acquired an interest in languages. At any rate, he became skilled in Latin, Greek, French, German, and Italian at an early age.

At twenty-one, Hodgkin began his medical studies at Guy's Hospital. He then took his M.D. degree at Edinburgh, the best medical school in Britain at that time owing to **Hermann Boerhaave's** influence on its teachers. Not content with this background, Hodgkin traveled to Paris for further studies and was able to learn the use of the newly invented stethoscope from the inventor himself, **René Théophile Hyacinthe Laënnec.** When he tried to introduce the instrument to his British colleagues, however, many of them sneered at the "newfangled contrivance."

Hodgkin settled in London. His shyness may have contributed to the slow growth of his practice. At any rate, he never had many patients. He practiced much at Guy's Hospital and was appointed curator of its museum of pathological cases after he was licensed by the London College of Physicians. He improved the museum and cataloged its collection. Hodgkin believed doctors could learn a great deal from the careful study of those who had died. From his observations, he gave lectures in morbid anatomy, that is, pathology. His studies led him to publish a two-volume work on the "morbid anatomy" of the membranes that secrete serum and mucous in the body. This was a valuable addition to medical literature, as was his treatise on swollen lymph glands and spleen, which first described Hodgkin's Disease from case studies. Hodgkin also worked closely with Joseph Jackson Lister (1786–1869) in studying and describing blood cells under J. J.'s newly improved microscope. Hodgkin showed that red blood cells are biconcave in shape and that in narrow capillaries these cells line up like stacked coins. Brilliant work such as this by Guy's trio of great doctors—Richard Bright (1789–1858), Thomas Addison (1793–1860), and Thomas Hodgkin—made the hospital one of the great medical schools of Britain.

His colleagues, however, did not reward Hodgkin's hard work and painstaking efforts. He desired an appointment at Guy's as Assistant Surgeon. Such an appointment would establish him in a settled income and open up opportunities to attract new patients to his private practice. Although he was a candidate for the position several times, his tendency to stand true to his observations, even when they contradicted men whose influence he needed, may have cost him his chance of appointment. After twelve years, he realized that he had no hope of obtaining the position at Guy's and moved over to St. Thomas's hospital. His private practice declined, and he devoted himself increasingly to charitable causes.

A generous man, Hodgkin did not press his patients for the fees they owed him. When a testimonial was raised in his honor, he insisted that the money go to charity.

Hodgkin's charity was a direct outcome of his faith. A Quaker, he moved in Quaker circles and was always zealous for the Society of Friends. As we have noted, he maintained Quaker speech and dress all of his life. His wife, Sarah Frances Scaife, made their home a center of hospitality, especially for fellow philanthropists. Not so well known is the fact that Hodgkin was an advisor to **Joseph Lister**, who discovered antiseptic surgery. Lister had fallen into depression, and Hodgkin advised him how to overcome this by the deliberate cultivation of a cheerful attitude.

Thomas Hodgkin was one of the founders of the Aboriginal Protection Society. With many other Quakers, he was ardent in his opposition to slavery. He denounced the practice of employing children as chimney sweeps. He recognized that overcrowding bred disease and advocated housing reform, better sanitation, fresh air, and exercise.

Among Hodgkin's charitable interests was concern for persecuted Jews. This sympathy brought him into close friendship with Sir Moses Haim Montefiore. Sir Moses was a philanthropist, related to the Rothschilds through marriage. In company with Montefiore, Hodgkin set out to tour the Holy Land. Unfortunately, Hodgkin contracted a severe case of dysentery in Jaffa and died before completing the expedition. Sir Moses raised a monument to his colleague in good causes. On it he inscribed the following words:

> Here rests the body of Thomas Hodgkin, M.D., of Bedford
> Square, London, a man distinguished alike for scientific

attainments, medical skill and self-sacrificing philanthropy. He died at Jaffa, the 4th of April, 1866, in the 68th year of his age, in the faith and hope of the Gospel.

17

John Story Kirkbride

(1809–1883)

Friend to the Insane

The tongue of the wise brings healing.
(Proverbs 12:18)

Of sixteen mental hospitals in the United States operating on a moral approach during John Kirkbride's life,
all were run by Protestants, several of them by Quakers.
Many of Kirkbride's principles—and theirs—were derived from William Tuke, a Quaker who had founded a
retreat for mental patients in York, England. Kirkbride
was merely the most notable of the American superintendents. Indeed, he became their unofficial spokesman.
He represents doctors of the mind.

One October morning in 1849, Doctor John Story Kirkbride, superintendent of the Pennsylvania Hospital for the Insane, was walking from his house to the hospital.

"There's someone up that tree," said his son, Joseph.

"Fetch the gatekeeper," said Kirkbride. He walked over to the tree, expecting to find an escaped inmate of the asylum.

The man in the tree spoke. Kirkbride recognized the voice. He knew at once that he was in grave danger and turned to run.

The man fired.

Pain exploded alongside the doctor's head.

Bravely, the gatekeeper rushed out and seized the assailant, one Wiley Williams.

Wiley Williams was indeed an escapee—from the year before. Cleverly, he had arranged a roll of clothes under his covers to make it look as if he were sleeping. He had set his nightcap where his head should be, crept into a rest room, and waited. As soon as the night watchman passed, fooled by the dummy, Wiley went over the wall and into the night. It was his second escape from the Pennsylvania Hospital for the Insane. For the second time, he returned to his family in Georgia. Although he was monomaniacal—a man dangerously driven by his focus on some single idea—his family agreed to keep him at home for a trial period. They were fearful of his eccentric behavior, which included threats, but they hoped he might have changed and were willing to see if he might do better this time outside the hospital.

Wiley was happy to have his freedom. He had hated the hospital and the man who ran it. He hated Kirkbride.

In April 1849, John Kirkbride received a letter from Wiley in which Wiley accused the superintendent of releasing others from the asylum but not him. The doctor had watched him closely while giving other patients less supervision and allowing them greater liberties. By holding him in the hospital, Wiley complained, Kirkbride had robbed him of friends, money, and happiness. He appointed himself Kirkbride's judge and executioner. "Thy death warrant is sealed," he wrote.

Kirkbride was a little disturbed. Wiley was, after all, a dangerous man. That is why he had been locked up. However, summer passed, and nothing happened. Kirkbride's uneasiness faded—until that cool October morning when Wiley shot him.

Kirkbride spent two weeks in bed before he could resume his duties. The bullet, deflected by his hat, had scraped the skull bone and come to rest in his scalp. The surgeon did not find it necessary to remove the lead, which could be felt from outside the wound when it healed. Wiley was tried. Characteristically, Kirkbride wrote to Wiley's father, "I can assure you in all sincerity that I should be as glad as ever to do anything that could be of service to him." Although he testified at Wiley's trial, it was only to establish that, in his opinion, Wiley acted while insane and was not responsible for his action. Kirkbride did not seek retribution. This was fitting for a man whose firm Christian beliefs taught him to forgive injuries. All the same, Wiley was deservedly awarded a life sentence as an insane criminal. He spent the rest of his days in Eastern State Penitentiary. John continued as superintendent of the Pennsylvania Hospital for the Insane.

John Story Kirkbride was born in 1809 near Morrisville, Pennsylvania. The son of Orthodox Quakers, he was a good-natured farm lad. Ninety-five percent of Americans were reared on farms in those days. John's body, however, was not strong enough for heavy farm labor. Clearly, he would have to engage in some other trade or profession. When his father fell seriously ill, John turned to the idea of becoming a doctor. Many Quakers became doctors. It was one of those solid, middle-class professions that they could conscientiously practice without violating the Bible's principles.

Since their emergence in England around 1650, the Society of Friends (Quakers) had shown themselves to be both practical and idealistic. Their practicality had made them shrewd and prosperous. Their Bible-based idealism had made them social innovators in such causes as prison reform, feminism, abolitionism, pacifism, the right to conscientious objection from military service, and the treatment of the insane. Kirkbride, who clung to conservative Quaker beliefs, was within the tradition of his faith when he became both a doctor and an asylum superintendent.

Pennsylvania was founded by William Penn as a refuge for persecuted Quakers. Quaker influence remained strong, although a split in the sect occurred in 1827. The Hicksites were Unitarian in outlook and tended to reduce Christ to a mere man. Significantly, the Kirkbrides sided with the conservatives who stressed sound doctrine, including Christ's redemptive power.

As a boy, Kirkbride expected to enter the medical profession. His father went to some expense to get him the best possible preparation. Like most doctors in early America, Kirkbride began his medical education as an apprentice to a private physician. Nicholas Belleville was a French doctor who had served the French contingent in the American revolutionary army. Nearing retirement, Belleville took Kirkbride as his last pupil. Belleville was an acute observer and taught his student to read physical signs in patients to diagnose their ailments. He advised prescribing no treatment if one could not identify the ailment. "If you do not know, nature can do a great deal better than you can guess." Kirkbride read and observed. From Belleville he learned the four-humors view of illness, which dated back at least to Hippocrates—400 B.C. Sickness was attributed to an imbalance of body fluids. Belleville employed bloodletting, emetics, purges, and natural drugs.

In the fall of 1828, Kirkbride entered Pennsylvania medical school. By attending formal school, he was becoming one of the best educated doctors in America. His medical education, however, was far behind that obtained at Edinburgh or Paris. The school had been heavily influenced by Benjamin Rush, a doctor who believed in violent remedies. By the time Kirkbride entered the school, theorists had decided that Americans were no longer the vigorous people they had once been. Rather than violent remedies, they needed remedies to build up their depleted systems. So Kirkbride was taught a gentler therapeutic approach that supported rather than fought against the body's efforts to throw off disease. He learned 110 drugs, including cathartics, diaphoretics, diuretics, emetics, enmenagogues, and narcotics. He learned to deliver babies, remove urinary tract stones, set bones, and perform joint surgery. His thesis was on neuralgia (acute pain along a nerve).

As a student, Kirkbride considered nervous irritation to be the cause of mental disorders. He believed that active pursuits and cheerful company were good remedies for a disturbed mind.

Today, most medical graduates are given residency privileges. This was not the case in Kirkbride's day. Few residencies were awarded, and, naturally, those few were bitterly contested. Upon graduation, Kirkbride gave up his chance of a residency at the Pennsylvania Hospital for a friend, hoping to take it the next year. Meanwhile, to broaden his experience, gain an income, and improve his chances of a residency, he took a position at the Friends Asylum for the Insane. The Pennsylvania Hospital for which he hoped to work also treated the insane, and he hoped that experience with the insane would be one more lever to help him pry open a coveted residency.

At the asylum, Kirkbride dealt with suicides and escapes as well as the usual gamut of mental illnesses. The asylum tried dealing with the insane through moral reeducation. However, their program had not worked well in practice. Recently, they had introduced drug therapies (such as opium) to supplement spiritual advice. In this medical-spiritual environment, Kirkbride made himself useful. Pleased, the asylum offered him a leadership position. He declined it to take up the residency at the Pennsylvania Hospital that was, indeed, offered to him. At the Pennsylvania Hospital, he again dealt often with the insane as well as with ordinary medical emergencies.

In 1836, Kirkbride opened his own practice. Patients he had met at the hospital came to him, but most of his efforts were for the poor. His income quickly rose to $500 a year, a considerable sum. He aimed at becoming a surgeon, for that was where real success lay.

But a surgeon he was not to be. John Paul, a member of the board of the Pennsylvania Hospital for the Insane, asked him to apply for the newly opened position of superintendent. The hospital had reorganized and was building a new facility outside the city. After some thought, Kirkbride agreed to apply. The position paid well, it would be influential, and he was beginning to doubt the ability of his frail body to sustain the demanding role of surgeon. Rather tentatively, he applied, was offered the job, and accepted it.

He took the job at a crucial moment in the history of mental institutions. Thanks to the pioneering efforts of men such as Philippe Pinel in France and the Tukes in England, treatment of the insane was improving. However, conditions were still appalling. In Philadelphia, for instance, the privilege of viewing patients was sold, and parties toured the asylums as a kind of freak show, staring at and baiting the wretched patients. Ideas on how to treat mental illness varied. Benjamin Rush was all for "heroic" measures—bleeding, gyrating, blistering, purging, and hot and cold showers. Others employed tranquilizer chairs to strap down a patient. One practitioner frightened a patient into a changed life with the threat of drowning. Others tried gentleness and claimed to effect cures through it.

Most boards and professionals who dealt with the insane believed that insanity was a moral problem. Few would deny that the body played a role. However, they thought that a disturbed spirit was especially vulnerable to mental as well as physical breakdown. They sought to convert their charges to faith in God. However, since so much mental illness took the form of religious mania, they wanted a sober approach to religion. Kirkbride's quiet faith, not revival enthusiasm, was what was needed.

Kirkbride read the literature and made his own observations before embarking on changes. The specialty was new. He infused it with a sense of mission. Quite naturally, he assumed the role of spokesman for his profession. No one more clearly articulated the moral view of treatment than he. He wrote a series of twenty-six propositions for treatment of the insane. For example, they were to be spoken to gently. A home-like atmosphere was to be maintained. Restraints were to be used only in emergencies.

Given great authority, Kirkbride used it with moderation. He removed shackles, except as temporary restraints for the most violent patients. The hospital was decorated as pleasantly as possible. He sought to hire assistants sharing his own Christian demeanor. His practice was to speak to each patient calmly and reassuringly, a practice that one former patient said "carries help and light to helpless, clouded minds." About half of his cases recovered. Even enemies of his religious philosophy and of his efforts to convert inmates to Christ spoke of him as "a gentleman noble and good as he is wise."

One of his patients was Eliza Butler. She came to him suicidal and depressed, feeling worthless. Kirkbride talked her through her gloomy thoughts and released her cured. Although she again had moments of gloom, she learned to submit her own will to God's will each time a lapse occurred.

Kirkbride's wife, Ann, died. She had been very sick for many years, but, as Kirkbride wrote, "bore all her sorrows with such perfect Christian resignation that her whole life has been a living sermon to all around her." Some years later, Kirkbride remarried. His choice was Eliza Butler.

Their marriage proved happy, and their four children all became outstanding citizens. Eliza taught Bible classes for Kirkbride's patients. Among the tasks Kirkbride set for Eliza was to compile the Bible's promises. Many patients tended to focus on the frightful warnings of Scripture. *Comforting Promises,* published in 1861, was intended to focus troubled minds on the most positive passages.

Under the law, Kirkbride did not have to allow patients to sue either him or the hospital. It was a measure of his character that he always voluntarily left open this avenue of redress, even when lawsuits became an annoyance to him. Patients were allowed to contact lawyers if they chose, and to bring suit even against him personally. His one precaution was to notify patients' families first.

After the Civil War, journalists, seeking sensational copy, attacked the asylums. Among their claims was a charge that asylums locked away sane individuals so that family members could plunder their money.

No doubt, the system had serious faults. Patients were housed in wards with characters who irritated them. Superintendents of Kirkbride's mind-set and exceptional ability were hard to find. So were Christian attendants with the patience to handle unruly patients and not retaliate when abused. A solitary superintendent could not spend enough time with each of the inmates who needed his attention. Too much power was vested in the superintendents. Mental illness was so difficult to define that it was hard to determine who was and who was not insane; under the system, wickedness and moral weakness could be confused with insanity.

Not surprisingly, then, even before Kirkbride's death, he saw the moral approach that he had championed largely abandoned. A new generation of doctors claimed that the Kirkbride method was unscientific and inhumane. Bureaucratic administrators took power. (It is inevitable that any political appointment will eventually fall into the hands of mediocrities.) With the coming of the new breed of rational administrators, a cult of pessimism swept the mental health community, producing profound doubt that the insane could be cured. Bereft of Kirkbride's love, cure rates declined. Those who accused the old system of inhumanity would have been horrified at the desperate remedies that followed. Lobotomies (cutting the frontal brain so that the left and the right sides no longer communicate), electroshock treatments, and brain-searing psychotropic drugs are but a few of the horrors introduced into mental health in the name of rationality and humanity.

Such methods would have been anathema to Kirkbride's Christian devotion. The character that led him to plead for his would-be assassin would never have permitted him to torture a recalcitrant inmate or to drug his or her mind beyond reception of the gospel. Eliza Butler Kirkbride wrote of her husband after his death that the secret of his success was "generous sympathy for all who suffer made manifest in his every thought and action."

18

James Young Simpson

(1811–1870)

Champion of Anesthesia

*God caused the man to fall into a deep sleep; and
while he was sleeping, he took one of the man's ribs
and closed up the place with flesh. (Genesis 2:21)*

Simpson was born for controversy. He had the boldness
of speech that characterizes the controversialist, and the
gut instinct to slug until victory was assured. Increasingly, with the development of chemistry, synthetic substances have been introduced into medicine. Simpson
was a formidable champion of one of the newly discovered drugs. He stands for the doctor who introduces
a chemical innovation to medicine.

A reporter once asked James Simpson to name his greatest discovery. The newsman expected, no doubt, to be given an example from anesthesia, obstetrics, or gynecology. Simpson's unexpected reply was, "When I found I was a sinner and that Jesus Christ was my savior." He said nothing of science and nothing of having served Queen Victoria as a personal physician. The important thing was Christ. That anecdote is a snapshot of the character of the great doctor.

Even as a boy, the youngest of seven sons, James Simpson seemed destined for greatness. He was so bright, so capable, so impressionable that his mother entrusted him with considerable responsibility, sometimes leaving him to handle the family bakery by himself before he reached his teens. In the local school, he was ahead of all the other pupils. The Simpsons were so impressed by his ability and determination that they stinted themselves to send him to a university, which he entered at the age of fourteen, "very young and solitary."

Two years later, he began medical studies and graduated in 1832, aged twenty-two. At graduation, his abilities were already widely recognized. Dr. John Thomson took him on as an assistant. Within a short time, he was lecturing in the good doctor's stead, illness having sidelined Thomson. Simpson continued his precocious ways. In 1835, aged twenty-five, he advanced beyond older doctors to become president of the Royal Medical Society of Edinburgh.

The midwifery chair came open. He applied for it and was told that it could be given to only a married man. Simpson left town and returned a month later, married to his distant cousin Jessie Grindby, for whom he had already exhibited more than a passing attachment. He got the job. Although he dedicated himself to his work and advanced the fields of obstetrics and gynecology, the job did not consume all his energies. Another interest would make his name more famous.

As a child, Simpson had been horrified by the cruelties he witnessed. For example, he saw a cow buried alive because it was believed to be the source of a recent plague. As a man, he was appalled by the torments inflicted on the ill in the name of healing. Such treatments included operating without anesthetics and the application of boiling tar to surgical wounds. When Dr. Morton made the first British demonstration of the use of ether in surgery, Simpson attended. He immediately adopted ether himself but found its effects unsatisfactory in part because it is highly flammable and therefore dangerous.

With the help of several doctors, he experimented on other soporifics. Eventually, he chanced upon chloroform. Three friends and he, sniffing it, became giddy. One by one, they slipped under the table. Simpson was delighted. He had found his ether substitute. He would use chloroform to ease women's childbearing pains and other medical torments. He rushed forward to tell the world of this new gift.

To his astonishment, he found himself attacked by theologians who protested that the use of anesthetic violates the Scripture that says women's pregnancy troubles would be greatly multiplied. These idealists argued that pain forces us into reliance on God. To relieve pain would make people haughty. Simpson countered Scripture with Scripture, showing that God put Adam to sleep before removing his rib. This biblical retort satisfied the public. It was legitimate to ease the pain of surgery. Chloroform, actually a dangerous anesthetic, came into widespread use until it was replaced by better chemicals.

Simpson was not idle in his chair. He advanced the techniques of caring for a woman's body. He showed how uterine sounds could be used to gain information about internal functions. For special procedures he introduced a sponge tent. He found new uses for the forceps. From his teaching, contemporaries learned better methods of removing ovaries. He studied and wrote on hermaphroditism. When Simpson rose to eminence, he used his authority to champion women who wanted to enter the field of medicine but were barred by millennia of prejudice.

Simpson became a member of many scientific societies and was widely honored. These honors seem to have gone to his head, for he became arrogant and exerted all of his influence against the antiseptic theories of **Joseph Lister**. The breach was aggravated by the outspokenness of the surgeon Dr. Syme, Lister's father-in-law, who had long been an adversary of Simpson. Needless suffering resulted.

Simpson advocated burning down buildings to destroy the agents of infection. The British medical establishment, unwilling to accept Lister in part because of Simpson's opposition, allowed "infected" buildings to be burned and paid no attention to Lister, even when he had proven his point beyond reasonable doubt.

Simpson was elevated to a baronetcy. Within days of his receipt of this honor, his oldest son died, followed a month later by his seventeen-year-old daughter. Of his nine children, five died before him. These blows shattered his health. He continued to work as long as he could but died May 6, 1870, at age fifty-nine.

A man much beloved by those who knew him best, he urged patient and student to trust in God. He knew the Bible from cover to cover. When the Scottish church split over issues of reform, he came out decidedly for the reformers. On his deathbed, he had his favorite psalms read to him. Despite his opposition to Lister, he was a man of faith who did much to relieve human misery.

19

James Paget

(1814–1899)

Innovative English Doctor

I pray that you may enjoy good health. (3 John 2)

It is possible to "look" at things without "seeing" them. Indeed, throughout most of history this appears to have been the practice of most people. James Paget was of that rare breed that looks *and* sees. He stands for all those doctors who have made original observations.

Your engagement in this profession binds you not only by consideration of your own interest but by weightiest responsibility to God and man to do your duty with all your might," wrote James Paget of medicine. "[D]aily remind yourselves that you propose to take in hand the lives and welfare of your fellow men—daily think quietly of what all this involves; and then you will daily decide that not even your own lives must be dearer to you than the duties of your profession."

As his words suggest, Paget was a committed Christian. During his London years, he demonstrated his commitment by walking a good distance each Sunday with his wife to St. Paul's Cathedral to attend church. In his writings and in an address to the English clergy titled "Theology and Science," he often alluded to his faith.

The eighth of seventeen children, Paget was the son of a ship-owning brewer, the mayor of Yarmouth. Educated originally at private school, he was apprenticed to Dr. Charles Costerton, a surgeon, when he was sixteen years of age. For four years, he performed menial tasks and prepared drugs for Costerton. The work was dull and included perhaps more accounting than anatomy, but Paget stuck it out and declared himself the better trained for it. He found a good deal of time to read and improved his medical knowledge through books and by close observation of the work of Costerton and other surgeons.

Believing that there could be "no true success without work," Paget diversified his efforts even while an apprentice. Already he was showing a flair for writing. He helped his brothers write a book on the natural history of the Yarmouth region. During the fifteen years after his graduation from St. Bartholomew's Hospital, he produced a leading journal article every two or three weeks for the *Medical Gazette*. He also wrote for the *Penney Cyclopedia* and translated medical works from several European languages in which he was essentially self-taught.

His entrance into St. Bartholomew's Hospital as a medical student came when he was twenty years of age. The quality of instruction was very low, he remembered later. "[T]here was nothing to encourage any kind of book learning." Anatomy was no better taught.

The dead-house (it was never called by any better name) was a miserable kind of shed, stone floored, damp and dirty, where all stood around a table on which the examinations were made. And these usually were made in the roughest and least instructive way; and, unless one of the physicians were present, nothing was carefully looked at, nothing was taught.

Paget, however, was a self-starter. Others might not read and might not observe, but he would. That first year at St. Bartholomew's Hospital, he noticed some little white specks in the muscles of a corpse and brought them to the attention of the teacher. "All the men in the dissecting rooms, teachers included, 'saw' the little specks in the muscles: but I believe that I alone 'looked at' them and 'observed' them." After some difficulty obtaining a microscope—he was one of the first to apply the microscope as an aid in the study of disease—he discovered the specks to be little worms that form cysts around themselves in the muscles: trichinosis.

Paget's diligence was rewarded. He was made curator of the hospital's anatomical museum. Although his pay was pitifully low, the duties were highly demanding. He was required to procure bodies for the anatomy students and to prepare specimens for surgical lectures. He was made demonstrator of anatomy.

Eventually, Paget was made full professor of anatomy and surgery. So respected was his instruction, his lectures were widely attended, not least because he had a knack for getting to the pith of any topic. Although his forte was diagnosis, he improved the treatment of bone and joint diseases. Paget's disease, *osteitis deformans,* a degenerative bone ailment, is named from his description. He described cancer of the nipple and the symptoms that sometimes precede it. He was made warden of the college of students. In other efforts, he catalogued the anatomical museum.

Many diligent men have gained prominence through medicine. So it was with Paget. Queen Victoria made him her surgeon extraordinary and raised him to a baronetcy. He also was elected a member of the Royal Society.

Paget's dealings were marked by modesty, punctuality, and honesty. This is borne out by his relationship with **Joseph Lister**, promoter of aseptic surgery, who developed his theories during Paget's life. When a conference of doctors seemed disposed to reject Lister's findings out of hand, Paget insisted that Lister receive a fair hearing. Paget himself tested the ideas, but he said that Lister's techniques did not work. He publicly rejected the aseptic theory. Years later, he anonymously observed Lister in surgery. After seeing for himself just how Lister performed the operations, he recognized that he had misapplied the great man's methods. It says much for Paget that he humbly apologized and publicly urged the adoption of Lister's lifesaving methods.

Many notable individuals were intimate friends of Paget. Among them were Cardinal Newman, Prime Minister Gladstone, poets Alfred Lord Tennyson and Robert Browning, author George Eliot, nurse Florence Nightingale, and many prominent scientists, including Darwin, Huxley, Pasteur, Virchow, and Koch.

Paget's family life was happy. His wife, Lydia North, assisted him by copying out his writing, sometimes until late at night. They had four sons and two daughters. Two of the sons, having acquired their father's strong religious convictions and careful observance of the requirements of his faith, became bishops. Modest and retiring, Paget attained his influence through careful work, sixteen-hour days, and the eloquent presentation of ideas. He died a year before the turn of the century, going to death without fear. One of his sons, the Bishop of Oxford, gave him the last consolation of the church. The nation honored him with a funeral service in Westminster Abbey.

The famed colorist John Everett Millais painted a likeness of Paget. It shows a man with a strong face and craggy features.

20

Joseph Lister

(1827–1912)

Antiseptic Surgeon

Rescue those being led away to death; hold back those staggering toward slaughter. If you say, "But we knew nothing about this," does not he who weighs the heart perceive it? (Proverbs 24:11–12)

Joseph Lister would make any list of top ten doctors. It is hard to imagine a gift greater than the aseptic surgery that resulted from his research. As is always the case with innovation, his ideas were fiercely resisted. He stands at the head of a long line of doctors who fought microbes.

Imagine yourself a young surgeon. Anesthetic has just come into use, and new surgical methods are being invented daily. Sweating under bright lights, you are assisting at one of the boldest operations so far attempted. Dozens of young doctors-in-training stare down at you under bright lights. If the operation goes wrong, the victim will die and a man will hang.

One of Joseph Lister's early operations, made as an assistant to his father-in-law, James Syme, followed just such a scenario. A man had been stabbed in the neck in a barroom brawl. The carotid artery, which bears blood to the brain, was nicked. Blood was pulsing into the neck. Policemen stood by to learn the outcome. If the patient died, the assailant would go on trial for murder. Needless to say, interest was intense. Joseph sweated profusely as he performed the careful operation. Fortunately, the victim lived.

The fact that Joseph Lister became a doctor was owing to his religion. He was born into a home of devout Quakers. Under English law, Quakers were barred from entering many schools either as students or as teachers. They could not, for instance, attend Cambridge or Oxford universities, which meant that they could not become lawyers. They could, however, engage in all trades and in medicine. Their plain habits and love of truth caused many of them to turn to science. Joseph's father, J. J. Lister, was an example. In addition to being a well-to-do wine distiller, he was an amateur scientist who succeeded in perfecting the compound microscope, eliminating aberration of images by employing two mutually corrective substances in the lens. With a family friend, the Quaker physician **Thomas Hodgkin**, J. J. Lister put his refined microscope to good use, sharing with Hodgkin the credit of being first to describe the true shape of a red blood cell. Young Joseph imbibed the faith, ambition, perseverance, and scientific inclination of his father. Before he turned sixteen, he had made many dissections under the microscope and announced his intention of becoming a surgeon. His single-minded determination was perfectly in accord with his solemn faith, which required hard work and implicit truth and forbade frivolities such as dancing.

Lister's devout mother was surprised. No one in the family had ever chosen to become a doctor. Yet she did not discourage her son. She had faithfully reared him and all of her other children, and if doctoring was his bent, she would not oppose it. Her doubt as to her son's aptitude for the profession (supposing she had doubts at all) must have been because he was kindhearted, shy, and stammering (perhaps because he had to dress and speak differently from others), and the profession with its horrible blend of pain and gangrene was not for the tenderhearted. As for his abilities, she had little doubt. He had been a steady, if not outstanding, pupil in Quaker school.

Once Joseph had made his decision, J. J. Lister did what he could to support it. He entered him into a "godless" college, London University, the only great institution in England that would not bar its doors to a Quaker. Later, Joseph wrote a grateful tribute to his father.

For a time, Joseph's future hung in doubt. Boarding with a melancholy Quaker, he lost the cheerfulness inculcated in him as a youth, becoming over-serious. He experienced a nervous breakdown following a mild case of smallpox. His father and the physician **Thomas Hodgkin** advised the young man to cast off introspection and cultivate a "pious, cheerful spirit." This Joseph did, touring Ireland to refresh himself. His sunny disposition returned and accompanied him the rest of his life.

Joseph entered upon his medical studies with a gift from his father: a microscope. It was not standard equipment in those days, but Joseph recognized its worth and applied it to his anatomical studies. While still a student, he authored a pamphlet, *Use of the Microscope in Medicine*, which may have encouraged other doctors to use that instrument in their studies.

Anesthetic had recently been invented. Surgical technique, as a consequence, was improving. But mortality rates from simple operations exceeded fifty percent, and no one understood why. It was because unsanitary conditions allowed microbes to be transferred from bed to patient, patient to patient, and doctor to patient. Conditions were so bad that **James Young Simpson**, the first doctor to use chloroform as an anesthetic, wrote that patients in hospitals were in more danger of imminent death than soldiers on battlefields.

The person who did as much as anyone to transform surgery from a gateway of death to a means of life was Joseph Lister. Not naturally talented as a surgeon, he found that he could achieve success through painstaking perseverance. In time, his slow, careful methods and use of "catgut" ligatures (which actually were the intestines of cows or sheep) became the norm.

In 1852, Lister graduated from University College, becoming a fellow of the Royal College of Surgeons. Determined to gain experience by observing the work of notable surgeons, he traveled to Edinburgh. There he became assistant to James Syme, one of the greatest surgeons of the day. Many students did not get along with Syme, who possessed a quick temper. Lister, however, did well with the great man, absorbed his technique—and married his daughter, Agnes. His proposed tour of surgeries never materialized. Lister's technique was so excellent that Syme soon relied on the young doctor in critical cases, such as the instance in which the man was stabbed in the carotid artery during a brawl.

Lister's marriage was happy. He and his wife worked side by side on experiments, often into the wee hours of the morning, and Lister's notes are as often in Agnes's hand as in his own. The two watched birds together. Such occupations filled a void, for they had no children. Because his wife was not a Quaker, Lister was compelled to leave the Society of Friends. He joined the Scottish Episcopal Church and remained a faithful churchgoer the rest of his life.

Eight years after he came to Edinburgh, Lister left to accept a professorship at the Glasgow Royal Infirmary. There he proved himself an innovative surgeon, pioneering many new surgical techniques and instruments. Throughout his life, he never ceased to invent surgical instruments and dressings, among them a hook to remove small objects from the ear, the screw tourniquet, and sinus forceps. Lister introduced the rubber drainage tube to British surgery. He also invented various glassware, a sterilizable syringe-pipette, and a hot box. All of these achievements would have ensured him a name of at least minor importance in the history of medicine. But his greatest achievement was yet to come.

Assigned a floor of the Glasgow hospital, he found atrocious death rates. Although he had not yet discovered antiseptic surgery, he thought that sanitary measures might reduce deaths. Over the opposition of the penny-pinching staff, he introduced such measures. Moreover, he renovated students' rooms and the lecture theater at his own expense. Despite his improvements in air circulation, cleanliness, and the provision of sick-room comforts, the death rate in his wards remained high, which troubled his Quaker-trained conscience. Why did so many patients die? Was there nothing the surgeon could do? What was the cause of infection? He had for many years studied tissues under the microscope and written about nerves, muscles, blood clotting and—most importantly—inflammation. His studies led him to believe that infection should not occur, and yet it did. But he simply could not learn why. With Quaker tenacity and Agnes's assistance, he persisted in his study.

He might never have found the answer had not a friend, Thomas Anderson, remembered his research interest and brought to his attention an article on fermentation written by Louis Pasteur (1822–1895). Lister, who read and spoke French, devoured the article. Immediately, he connected Pasteur's ideas about microbes with the infections so common to surgery. With Agnes, he repeated every one of Pasteur's experiments and convinced himself of their truth. Then he began a deliberate search for an antiseptic agent that might protect his patients from infection. In the north, a tar-like substance was being used to treat city sewage. This came to his attention. He determined that carbolic acid was the active agent in the tar. He first tried carbolic acid on an eleven-year-old boy who was run over by a cart and had a bone protruding through his skin. Lister tested carbolic acid on many more injuries, greatly lowering the death rate. Finally, he induced Britain's most prestigious medical journal, *The Lancet,* to print his discoveries. In a later paper, "On the Antiseptic Principle of the Practice of Surgery," he advocated the use of a solution of one part carbolic acid diluted in twenty parts of water.

Shortly, he was able to announce a drastic improvement in the death rates in his ward. Blood poisoning, gangrene, and infection fell dramatically. Compound fractures, which had previously required amputation, could now be set and healed.

Lister's careful research met with howls of derision. Almost to a man, British doctors rose to jeer the suggestion that they, the physicians, had been the culprits in their patients' deaths when, with filthy hands and clothes, they had introduced germs into the wounds they had meant to heal. **James Young Simpson**, the lion of British physicians, should have allied himself with Lister. Instead, he became a powerful foe. This opposition stemmed, in part, from an ancient rivalry with Lister's hot-tempered father-in-law, Syme. How often wounded pride blinds the mighty.

In spite of such high-placed opposition, however, Lister persevered. He continued to publish studies on his techniques and their results. Students who sat under this gentle, determined teacher began to carry his new techniques into the world. If he was ignored as a prophet in his homeland, he was followed in Europe. Appalled at the casualties in their latest war, the Germans, especially, were desperate enough to try anything. They tested Lister's methods. Success stories began to trickle back to England. Eventually, British physicians came around to the new methods, although London's surgeons held out bitterly. In the United States, William W. Keen (1837–1932) promulgated Lister's antiseptic surgery.

Lister continued to promote his new methods. He was very practical, meeting a need wherever he found it. The story has often been told how he found one of his small charges weeping. Her doll had been taken from her by a nurse who was fearful of contamination because it leaked sawdust. Knowing that possession of a doll would improve the girl's chance of recovery by comforting her, Lister fetched the toy and performed "surgery," restoring it to her sewn up.

In 1877, Lister's practicality caused him to take a dramatic step. He left Edinburgh, where he was successful and admired, and moved to London, where he was denounced and despised. London remained the hotbed of opposition to his ideas. Since London's physicians seemed determined to misunderstand his methods, Lister decided that he would demonstrate them in the stronghold of his opponents. To his chagrin, he found that students, prejudiced by entrenched teachers, refused to attend his classes. With stalwart perseverance, he persisted. He would prove his point by demonstrating success in cases that the greatest London surgeons would blanch to handle. For instance, he wired together a fractured kneecap, a process which in the old days would inevitably have resulted in festering gangrene. Lister's gamble paid off. **James Paget**, a prominent London surgeon who years earlier urged his colleagues to lend Lister an ear but then repudiated him because he misunderstood his procedures, reversed himself and adopted Lister's methods after seeing the master in operation with his own eyes. The surgeons could not argue with visible success.

Many awards were poured upon Lister in his old age. At the triennial meeting of the International Congress of Medical Science in Amsterdam, he was cheered wildly by crowds and again at a theater later, where he was recalled by ovations three times. The fact that he was raised to a baronetcy and became the first physician to sit in the House of Lords meant little to him, however, when his adored Agnes died. The two had lived in deep accord for more than thirty-five years, and something died in Lister with her passing. Nonetheless, he continued with his duties, eventually becoming president of the Royal Society.

The friendship between Pasteur and Lister is well known. When Pasteur was an old man, suffering the results of stroke, Lister attended Pasteur's jubilee, and the two embraced. Pasteur died three years later.

At his own death in 1912, Lister was deeply mourned by a nation that had universally adopted his techniques, having learned from his work with antiseptics to avoid sepsis. The grateful nation wished to inter him in Westminster Abbey, but Lister's will requested that he be laid beside Agnes.

All of Lister's biographers agree on his character. Medical biographer Nuland says, "There was a flavor of simple goodness in his life, flowing evenly from the philosophical spring of a distinctive faith that has nourished the spirit of more than a few of the moral leaders of the past 300 years."

He was gentle, quick to apologize if anything he wrote gave offense. No one heard him raise his voice in anger. He was not even impatient with his detractors. Not one flaw has been attributed to him, except a lack of punctuality, which was usually due to some experiment. Once he delayed an urgent operation for two hours while he butchered a heifer and tested a new technique. He then used the technique in the very operation he had kept waiting.

Lister wrote of his faith, "I am a believer in the fundamental doctrines of Christianity." Just what this meant to him as a doctor can best be summarized in words he spoke to a graduating class: "It is our proud office to tend the fleshly tabernacle of the immortal spirit, and our path, if rightly followed, will be guided by unfettered truth and love unfeigned. In pursuit of this noble and holy calling I wish you all God-speed."

21

Clara Swain

(1834–1910)

Asia's First Woman Medical Missionary

*Heal the sick, raise the dead, cleanse those who have
leprosy, drive out demons. Freely you have received,
freely give. (Matthew 10:8)*

Clara Swain was a trailblazer. One of the first in a generation of women doctors, she was a pioneer in taking medical care to women in India, founding a nursing school
that demonstrated the value of Christian medical mis-
sions as a means of reaching the subcontinent for Christ.
Her life exhibits the woman as a pioneer in medicine.

In 1869, Reverend D. W. Thomas called for a woman doctor for Bareilly, India. A woman could go where a man could not, he said, and open doors for the gospel. Many Indian women, especially those of higher castes, lived highly restricted lives, curtailed because they were not allowed to show themselves to any man outside the immediate family. Even the services of a male doctor were forbidden to them. Aroused by his plea, the Ladies Union Missionary Society offered to fund the position.

One doctor who heard the appeal was Clara Swain. It piqued her interest, and she began to pray. For three months, she pondered and prayed. At last, her mind was settled. God was calling her to India. A life of foreign adventure was about to open for her.

Had Clara been born just half a century earlier, she could not have answered the appeal. At her birth in 1834, not a single American woman had graduated from medical school. Elizabeth Blackwell's (1821–1910) landmark achievement came when Clara was fourteen. It was still so rare for a woman to go into medicine that Clara did not even consider the field as a career for herself until a woman physician, falling seriously ill, wrote of the desperate need for women doctors. After deep prayer—Clara was a praying woman—she believed that the Lord would have her go into medicine. She entered medical college at a time when a female medical student still drew stares and raised eyebrows.

One of the first American schools to admit women was the Women's Medical College of Pennsylvania. Quaker influence had something to do with that. The Quakers were among the first of the post-Reformation denominations to admit women to full equality with men. Having completed her degree in 1865, Clara was working at a sanitarium when she learned of India's plight.

Clara recognized that she would be breaking new ground. A few men had done medical missionary work in India (despite resistance from their boards), but she would be the first woman to do so. The obstacles might have seemed daunting, but her portrait shows a woman with a determined jaw. Having arranged to work under the newly organized American Methodist Episcopal Mission, rather than the Ladies Union Missionary Society, Clara sailed with Isabella Thoburn in November 1869.

Through Christmas the weather was not bad, but the rough weather she experienced near the end of her journey left her with little love for the sea. "I was too sick to write," she recalled, "and I had five sick ones to look after besides myself as there was no stewardess or ship doctor. I cannot bear to think of the sea, it treated me so badly."

"My medical work began the day of my arrival," wrote Clara in her book, *A Glimpse of India.* Her medical supplies had not yet reached Bareilly. But with characteristic decisiveness, she did not let that deter her, making do with what she could borrow. She treated fourteen patients that first day. Her boxes did not arrive for another month. Just ten days later, she opened her school of nursing. Her students were orphans and three married women. The school of nursing was a first for India's women and created quite a stir among the British and the Indians alike. Lieutenant Governor Sir William Muir and Lady Muir came to investigate for themselves. Indian leaders also visited the mission.

Clara taught everything: anatomy, obstetrics, physiology, *materia medica,* and diseases of women and children. In addition to her duties as teacher, she treated thirteen hundred patients. Twice a week, she took her students to nearby villages to treat illness on-site. "Nearly everyone in our mission is really overworked," she wrote. When her first class graduated in 1873, she did not attempt a second. Even with her strong will, she felt unable to repeat so arduous a course of action. Nonetheless, her success, recounted in lively letters home, drew other women doctors to India. Thanks to Clara, one of those women, Doctor **Ida Scudder**, found the path for women medical missionaries well trodden by the time she built the Vellore women's medical college.

The need for a clean, comfortable hospital for her patients and nurses was apparent to Clara early on. To obtain the land, she had to appeal to the nawab at Rampore. The nawab, a Muslim, had declared that no Christian missionary would ever be allowed into his city. Clara determined to visit him anyhow and win his permission. She traveled to Rampore. The nawab would not see Clara and her little party the first day. Clara was grateful for the delay; the additional hours allowed her to kneel in fervent prayer. The next morning, the nawab provided them with a breakfast of twenty-four dishes. As Clara approached his palace, his subjects salaamed and cried, "Long life!"

Mr. Thomas, Clara's interpreter, requested the land for a hospital. "Take it, take it," exclaimed the nawab. "I give it with pleasure for such a purpose." Christ had prevailed.

Clara built her hospital like a hotel so that the castes could maintain full privacy. Prescription cards were printed with gospel verses on the back in Arabic, Hindu, Persian, and Roman characters. Since patients usually were accompanied by many family members, Clara seized this as an evangelistic opportunity. She trained women to read to everyone who would listen and offered classes in sewing, reading, and knitting.

Clara did not consciously seek adventures, but they came her way all the same. In 1880, the year she returned to India from a four-year health furlough, violent rains during the wet season burst through her window and washed away her baggage. She and several associates fled to a nearby house. They had to flee again shortly after when the waters also devoured that structure. As houses fell around them, they considered dashing to refuge in assembly rooms on a nearby hill. Moments later, before they could make their dash, they watched a mud slide demolish those very rooms with the loss of 250 lives. Thousands more died in the swollen Ganges.

Another adventure nearly decapitated her. "My native assistant and I mounted the elephant and just as we were passing out of the yard, the driver said we must lower our heads or we would get hurt. The yard was enclosed by a high wall and had a gate fifteen feet high with a beam across the top. I thought my head was as low as I could get it, but the beam caught me under the chin and at the side of my head. My assistant screamed and the driver backed the elephant at once thus saving my head but it was black and sore for some days."

In 1885, Clara turned fifty-one. Sixteen years had brought her considerable recognition in India, but her health had suffered seriously. The chance to become palace doctor to the Rani of Ketri proved congenial to her. It would reduce her workload. With her inveterate habit of prayer, she gave the move much consideration and con-cluded that it was a door she might as justly enter as someone else. The royal family made her most welcome and later relinquished her services only with great reluctance. "We find the Rajah and Rani most interesting people, noble and generous, and so kind and con-siderate that we can hardly realize they are not Christians," she wrote. "If we might only be the means of bringing them to Christ, how glad I should be!"

Her prayers were partly answered when the Rajah agreed to allow the doctor to instruct his daughter and other girls in the Christian faith. Clara found many superstitions to overcome. One girl wanted to wor-ship Clara's sewing machine. Such a useful object must be worthy of adoration! Because priests taught that females would be punished by the gods for learning to read, the women were hesitant to imbibe for-bidden knowledge. Clara managed to overcome this superstition in many cases. What appalled Clara most, however, was that Indians killed their girl babies with no sense of wrongdoing. She tried by edu-cation to discourage this dreadful practice.

By 1896, Clara's health had deteriorated to the point that she could no longer remain in India. She returned to the United States. She was not quite done with India, however. In 1906, she was able to revisit the land of her labors for a mission Jubilee. To her delight, she found that the people remembered her with great affection.

Clara died Christmas Day, 1910. Her greatest adventure had begun.

22

Walter Reed

(1851–1902)

Conqueror of Yellow Fever

Let us not become weary in doing good, for at the
proper time we will reap a harvest if we do not give up.
(Galatians 6:9)

Walter Reed stands for the modern epidemiologist—
the person who discovers the cause of an epidemic and
undertakes practical measures for battling it.

W alter Reed Hospital. It is often in the news, that imposing military hospital in Washington, D.C. How many of us know anything of the Christian man after whom it was named—a doctor of quality and grit who freed the United States and Cuba of one of the most dangerous pestilences that ever troubled mankind?

Yellow fever was a seasonal scourge to the nation, a semitropical nightmare that left up to 85 percent of its victims dead. During the Spanish-American War, it killed more men than bullets did. By a well-conducted series of experiments, Walter Reed demonstrated that the *Aëdes aegypti* mosquito was the carrier of the disease. In doing so, he confirmed the key point of the theories of the Cuban doctor Carlos Finlay, who had suggested mosquitoes as the carrier. Reed, a notable bacteriologist and army surgeon, also did original work on typhoid.

God employs willing hands as His own. From early childhood, Reed, already a practicing Christian, prayed to be used by God in some capacity by which he might better the lot of others.

He came naturally to faith. His father, Lemuel, was a Methodist minister. Throughout his childhood, Reed moved every two years when his father moved: Belroi, Princess Anne City, Murfreesboro, Farmville, Bedford, and Blackstone. He was in Blackstone during much of the Civil War. Sent to hide the family horses, he took them among the trees by a river. As he prepared for a swim, Yankee raiders appeared, capturing him and confiscating the horses. He walked ignominiously home to his frightened parents. An elder brother, Jim, had joined the army and lost an arm in battle.

Walter's childhood was full of fun and pranks. His father, who often wrestled with his sons, was an understanding man. For instance, when Walter poisoned himself on tobacco at six years of age, the father asked who had given him the weed. Walter would not say, and his father wisely commended him for his loyalty to his friends. With this kind of upbringing, the lad was good-humored and conscientious.

Fortunately for Walter's education, his father obtained a church at Charlottesville. At a local institute, Lt. William R. Abbott impressed the young man with his fiery teaching. Reed thrived.

After the war, many Southerners were driven by the desire to re-build the ruined South, and Walter determined to become a doctor. At fifteen, he entered the University of Virginia, where some of the South's noblest minds taught. He sought to take his bachelor degree after only a year. Although he wasn't allowed to do so, he negotiated a compromise that let him earn his medical degree in two years. At that time, a medical degree was awarded to anyone who could pass the rigorous exam. The committee agreed to let him try. Grinding at his studies night and day, the youth achieved the goal.

Book learning is fine in its own way, but Walter wanted practical experience and went to New York in search of it. In the great city, he took a second M.D. degree at Bellevue Hospital Medical College. He labored among the poor, became an assistant physician, and was appointed health inspector. Always sensitive, he is said to have looked at each person as a human being and not as a "case."

Medicine could not prevent his noticing the opposite sex. One girl in particular caught his eye—Emilie Lawrence. About the time that he fell in love with her, he determined to enter the army as a doctor. This might seem a lowly aim for a man of ambition, but Reed believed that he was destined to be more than a mere outpost medic, that Providence had great things in store for him. His faith exhibited itself in prayer, as when he mentioned in a letter that he was praying for Emilie's sick nephew. "Alas, while I prayed that his life might be prolonged to many years of usefulness, he had already departed for a better and brighter home." The boy had escaped the evil of the world, he thought. "And for this ought we not rather to bless His Holy Name than yield to unavailing grief?"

Told to report to Arizona, he asked for prior approval to return for his wedding. "Young man, if you don't want to go to Arizona, resign from the service," the Surgeon General of the Army brusquely told Reed.

Reed pulled himself up with spirit. "General, I did not labor for my commission with all the will which I did to throw it away hastily, nor can you deprive me of it until I act so unworthily as to cause dismissal." Impressed, the general offered Reed a cigar and chatted with him. In the end, however, he denied Reed's request. With characteristic decisiveness, Reed married Emilie at once. This act took courage on her part, too, for she knew she was going to have to follow him alone into the Wild West to meet him and then accompany him on all his moves there.

Reed departed for his post. Emilie set out to join him a year later. During her journey to San Francisco, where Walter was to meet her, she encountered a blizzard and was in a train collision. The trip to San Francisco required but a week. Her trip with Walter to Arizona took another twenty days and included being lost in the dark their first night! The young bride and groom moved from base to base despite arduous difficulties. They were rewarded with interesting incidents. For example, Reed treated Geronimo and his Indian troops in Nebraska. Throughout the next eleven years, Reed kept up with new medical discoveries as best he could by studying the trickle of journals and articles that reached the frontier surgeries. At times, he duplicated the experiments about which he read.

Transferred back East thirteen years later, he was allowed to study pathology at Johns Hopkins and made the most of his opportunity. One of the notable doctors at that great hospital was **Howard A. Kelly**. The two later shared a correspondence. The Surgeon General of the Army forbade Reed to study bacteriology, declaring it a useless subject. For two years more, Reed cooled his heels in another outpost. The Surgeon General died unexpectedly and was replaced by the forward-looking Sternberg, who made Reed an educator in the army medical school in Washington, D.C. There, the eager soldier studied typhoid, making significant discoveries. An enthusiastic nephew, learning that Uncle Walter needed white rats for his experiments, bred and sent him so many that Reed had to order a stop to the deliveries.

In 1896, Reed was able to show that neither swamp water nor food was responsible for malaria. But, like most of his contemporaries, he attributed the disease to "bad air."

During the Spanish-American War, typhoid broke out. The army refused to acknowledge the plague, but Reed and others served on a board that confirmed it. Although the bacillus was found in drinking water, they showed that flies and contact with feces were the principle transmitters. The board members learned the incubation period of the disease, developed life-saving sanitary measures, and insisted on the practical step of installing screens to reduce the number of germ-carrying flies in barracks and tents.

Yellow fever was also a big killer during the war. Most experts thought the disease was transmitted by "fomites," small contaminated particles. Reed thought so, too. One man who did not think so was Dr. Carlos Finlay of Havana.

Named to a board charged to solve the yellow-fever problem once and for all, Reed and his colleagues Carroll, Lazear, and Agramonte set out to locate the bacillus. They could not find it. They later learned that the disease agent is viral, too small to be seen with optical microscopes.

Reed's studies seemed to point to mosquitoes as the carriers of the disease, confirming Finlay's theory. In a dangerous move, Lazear attached mosquitoes to potential victims. At first, no one caught the disease, and the doctors were discouraged. Later knowledge revealed that an incubation period was needed. Eventually, Dr. Carroll contracted yellow fever, apparently from a mosquito bite. He survived, as did a private who got the disease from the experiments. Lazear experimented on himself, caught the disease, and died. This tragedy was allowed to appear to be an accident, apparently for fear that the Lazear family would not be able to collect life insurance if the voluntary nature of Lazear's test became known.

As these controlled cases multiplied, the facts of transmission became clearer. Reed devised a brilliant double experiment in which groups of volunteers lived in yellow fever filth for several weeks, some groups carefully screened from mosquitoes and other groups exposed to mosquitoes. He also tested direct infection by injection. The tests on the brave volunteers proved beyond a shadow of doubt the nature of transmission. The skill of the commission saved all of the volunteers who contracted the disease.

Reed did not live long to bask in his great discovery. Just fifty-one, he died of appendicitis. But his prayer had been answered: he had accomplished something worthwhile for others. In memory of his character and genius, Walter Reed Hospital was named for him.

Lazear should be honored, too, for he gave his life in the search. These men and the other noble volunteers saved the world incalculable misery and, as a bonus, eased the building of the Panama Canal.

Walter Reed was ever a man of faith. His letters often refer to the heavenly Father. "Once more the God of day has chased away the clouds and we are happy." "A thousand Happy New Years for my sweet wife and son! God bless and preserve you both is ever the prayer of your fond and devoted husband."

Kelly, Reed's biographer, wrote that Christian principle was a distinguishing trait of the conqueror of yellow fever. The greatest lesson to be learned from Reed's life is that happiness and usefulness lie in giving what we can to life rather than getting what we can from it. In the book *Microbe Hunters*, Paul De Kruif called Reed a blameless man, "mad to help his fellowmen." Our national institutions should be named for such men.

23

Ronald Ross

(1857–1932)

Malaria's Conqueror

It is not good to have zeal without knowledge, nor to be hasty and miss the way. (Proverbs 19:2)

Ronald Ross represents the doctor who, through original investigation, earns high distinction and awards. His work traced the cycle of malaria through mosquito to man and back again. It won him a Nobel prize.

Ronald Ross won the Nobel prize for his work on malaria. The award was controversial. To begin with, the hypothesis that mosquitoes transfer malaria to humans was not Ross's own idea but the suggestion of tropical specialist Patrick Manson. Then, after Ross made his brilliant discoveries, he did not make them watertight. Giovanni Battista Grassi (1854–1925) eventually provided elements of proof. Priority disputes also arose because other researchers, especially Alphonse Laveran (1845–1922), had anticipated or independently duplicated portions of Ross's work.

Ironically, the future Nobel prize winner resisted the idea of becoming a doctor—even while attending medical school! His passions were music and literature. He churned out unheard symphonies, unplayed dramas, and unread sagas by the dozens. Verses flowed from his pen. All of them were unsuccessful. Ronald was finally motivated into action by a warning. His father, a general in the Indian armies and the sire of nine other children besides Ronald, threatened to cut off his son's allowance because of his desultory study habits. So Ronald took a position as ship's surgeon, boned up on his neglected medical studies while at sea, passed the Indian Medical Service exam, and settled into work.

At first, his duties were light. He found time for his favorite pursuits of music, literature, and erratic studies. He turned his hand to everything that interested him: mathematics, *Principias* of the universe, shorthand systems, phonetic schemes, and surgery. In everything he failed to make a lasting mark. But then he met and married Rosa Bloxam. His responsibility as husband sobered him. "I was neglecting my duty in the medical profession," he later wrote. "I was doing my current work, it was true; but what had I attempted toward the betterment of mankind by trying to discover the causes of those diseases which are perhaps mankind's chief enemies?" During an 1888 furlough to England, he buckled down to some serious study and acquired his diploma in public health. He also took a class in bacteriology.

Back in India, Ross studied malaria. Unable to find the crescent-shaped larvae with black granules that Alphonse Laveran had documented in 1880, Ross wrote four papers deriding the theory of mosquito transmission advanced by Patrick Manson (1844–1922). He claimed, instead, that malaria was an intestinal problem.

Patrick Manson set him right. In 1894, Ross visited London again, and Manson showed Ross under the microscope that Laveran was correct in identifying black-granuled crescents in malaria victims. He urged upon Ross the notion that mosquitoes were, indeed, the carrier. Ross did an immediate flip-flop. Sensing a chance to immortalize his name with a scientific discovery, he returned to India, leaving Rosa and his children in the motherland while he sleuthed for the culprit. Among the many questions he needed to answer were these: Which of the world's many mosquitoes carried the disease? Where in the mosquito were the black crescents to be found?

Three years of difficult research followed. Ross was hampered by lack of access to scientific journals. He did not know, for example, that A. F. A. King had also suggested that malaria was transmitted by mosquito bites. Ross was also impeded by official displeasure. Just as the Surgeon General of the United States Army had derided **Walter Reed's** interest in bacteriology, so Ronald Ross's superiors sniffed at his "waste" of time. At crucial moments in the malaria cycle, they ordered him to other tasks, setting back his research. Once they even transferred him to a region where malaria was rare.

At one point, Ross was near despair. He had dissected unsuccessfully hundreds of mosquitoes of hundreds of breeds. He had even dissected the right mosquito without knowing it. Precious samples had died. He began the dissection of yet another *anopheles* mosquito.

I went carefully through the tissues, now so familiar to me, searching every micron with the same passion and care as one would search some vast ruined palace for a little hidden treasure. Nothing. No, these new mosquitoes also were going to be a failure; there was something wrong with the theory. But the stomach tissues still remained to be examined—lying there, empty and flaccid, before me on the glass slide, a great white expanse of cells like a large courtyard of flagstones, each one of which must be scrutinized—half an hours work at least. I was tired, and what was the use? I must have examined the stomachs of a thousand mosquitoes by this time. But the angel of fate fortunately laid his hand on my head; and I had scarcely commenced the search again when I saw a clear and almost perfectly circular outline before me of about 12 microns in diameter. . . .

I remember opening the diaphragm . . . of the microscope to admit more light and then changing the focus. In each of these cells there was a cluster of small granules, black as jet, and exactly like the black pigment granules of the Plasmodium crescents.

That night, he scribbled a few lines of a poem, quoting the apostle Paul's triumphant lines on resurrection and immortality:

> I know that this little thing
> A million men will save—
> Oh, death, where is thy sting?
> Thy victory, oh, grave?

It was August 20, 1897. Later, in addition to identifying the mosquito that carried malaria, Ross found the parasite it transmitted, traced the life cycle of the parasite, and discovered the means of its transmission. His study was aided by a curious fact: birds also contract malaria. By studying malaria in avians, he was able to conduct controlled experiments. Eventually, he learned that malaria is transmitted not by *ingestion,* as he had supposed, but by the *bite* of an infected mosquito.

Proof that malaria was transmitted by mosquitoes was of utmost importance. It allowed preventative measures to be taken, measures that met with success wherever they were tried. If mosquito eggs were killed and if door and window screens denied the pests entry into the home, malaria could be reduced. Ross became a champion of such methods. In Cuba, Walter Reed benefited from Ross's trailblazing researches when he undertook his study of yellow fever, a disease also transmitted by mosquitoes.

Ross was restless and impatient. He often stopped work when just one experiment more could have ensured his success. He wanted very much to be important, to sit on committees. In the end, he did—committees dealing with tropical medicine.

And he won the Nobel prize. Laveran would also win the Nobel for his work in tropical diseases. But it was Ross who found the crucial clue that made all subsequent research on the subject "mere child's play which anyone could do after the clue was once obtained."

He turned to God with gratitude when he made his discovery. One verse of his victory hymn, full of exaltation despite its doggerel, read:

> He is the Lord of light
> He is the thing that is;
> He sends the seeing sight
> And the right mind is his.

24

Howard Atwood Kelly

(1858–1943)

Johns Hopkins's Fourth

The heavens are Thine, the earth also is Thine;
The world and all it contains, Thou hast founded them.
(Psalm 89:11 NASB)

Kelly stands for the doctor whose command of his specialty united with humility to bring him the respect of all his associates. He was an author of medical textbooks and trainer of other doctors. His network of influence was immeasurable.

I dedicate myself—my time—my capacities—my ambition—everything to Him. Blessed Lord, sanctify me to Thy uses. Give me no worldly success which may not lead me nearer to my Savior." So wrote Howard Atwood Kelly the night he took his medical degree.

These words were not a passing whim. Kelly could have written them at any time between his childhood and old age. His was a consistent Christianity. Some of his earliest diary entries record his determination to live a godly life. His last utterance was, "Nurse, bring me my Bible." From the age of thirteen (when he was confirmed at his own request) until his death, he always carried a New Testament with him and shared its words with others as occasion permitted. Christianity stamped all of his actions as a doctor and marked his relationship with the other great doctors of Johns Hopkins, with his pupils, and with his friends.

At first, Kelly did not intend to pursue a medical career. He had set his sights on becoming a naturalist. As a youth, he developed a deep interest in snakes, turtles, bugs, and butterflies. Snakes continued to fascinate him throughout his life, and many stories were told of his delight in them. When the other boys fled their swimming hole in a snake-induced panic, he dived in and caught the wriggling serpent, showing them that it was not a dreaded water moccasin but a harmless water snake. After he became famous, more than one gaggle of guests fled in panic from the snakes that had escaped in his library. His cook had to be wheedled into staying when an escaped snake startled her out of the kitchen.

As a teenager, Kelly received a helping hand from Edward Drinker Cope (1840–1897), a friendly paleontologist who taught him the rudiments of fossil classification. Kelly boiled animals down to their bones and extracted their skeletons. On his own initiative, he studied the languages of naturalism, German and French. Cope sponsored Kelly for membership in the Academy of Sciences, and the boy was delighted to win acceptance. Now he could borrow books from the academy library and teach himself even more about nature. He tramped about the countryside, collecting specimens he'd seen described in books. To acquire even more natural lore, he set out on foot from Philadelphia with a friend to visit Niagara Falls and Canada, killing a large rattler en route.

Despite these interests, however, he did not become a professional naturalist. His father pointed out how few jobs were available in that field and urged his son to take up some other profession. Because of the close connection between the subject matter of naturalism and medicine, Kelly chose medicine. Perhaps his choice was foreshadowed in childhood.

As a boy, Kelly disappeared one day. When he did not come home that night, his mother was frantic with worry. He returned home the next day, bubbling with excitement. He had slipped off to watch an autopsy! He learned a sterner lesson—to tell his mother where he was going. On future expeditions, he wrote her frequent letters to spare her anxiety.

Kelly's father provided him with a microscope when he entered medical school. As strange as it might sound, this tool was still not yet standard equipment. Students crowded into Kelly's home to peer through the eyepiece just as they had crowded around **Joseph Lister**, who alone in his class possessed a similar precious instrument. In medical school, Kelly did not limit himself to the required class work. He maintained all of his old interests. So intent was he on mastering his subjects that he was at work from eight in the morning until ten at night every day.

The medical course was for three years. Two months before graduation, Kelly suffered a severe setback. His overstimulated mind would allow him no sleep. He had to drop out of school. To regain his health, he worked on a cattle ranch in Colorado for a year. Gradually, his mind rested, and he developed a powerful physique. At the same time, he tended injuries and delivered his first baby.

Once his insomnia was gone, Kelly returned to school. He would study hard until the end of his life, but he learned to vary his pursuits as a means of relaxation so that he would not suffer sleeplessness again.

Henry Kelly saw his son graduate. Proudly, he outfitted a room for his boy's home practice. But to Kelly medicine could never be merely a means of income. Already he had decided that his real work, given free if need be, must be among the poor of Kensington, a suburb of Philadelphia. To avoid hurting his father's feelings, he shared his practice between home and Kensington, but Kensington soon won out. There he converted a house into his own private hospital. He also helped his sister establish in Kensington a mission work known as The Lighthouse. Over the years, he backed this work financially.

Kelly found his specialty in gynecology. He discovered new techniques for diagnosing gynecological problems. He invented a widely imitated surgical drop light and a method of dressing incisions, which came into universal use. In due time, he contributed to the improved treatment of stones, fibroids, cancers, rectal tears, vaginal fistulas, and other gynecological complaints. Consultations brought him into continual contact with the greatest doctors of Philadelphia, including William Osler (1849–1919). He acquired a reputation among his fellow doctors for his boldness, quickness, and brilliance. They generally acknowledged him as the greatest master of surgical technique of the day.

In 1868, the University of Pennsylvania offered Kelly a professorship. He accepted, but a year later he moved on.

Johns Hopkins (1795–1873) was a wealthy Quaker merchant of Baltimore. At his death, he willed seven million dollars to endow a university hospital. William Osler recommended Kelly as head of the department of gynecology. Kelly was just thirty-one. With William Osler, William Welch (1850–1934), and William Halsted (1852–1922), he became the fourth member of the best-known medical teaching team ever assembled in America, memorialized in a famous painting done by John Singer Sargent. The other three were somewhat older than Kelly. Osler loved to use Kelly's age against him. Slipping into the wards ahead of Kelly, he would warn the patients not to worry about the senile tremor in Kelly's hand. "It disappears when he begins to operate," he told them. Of course, this advance notice led patients to expect an old man and made it hard for Kelly to convince his patients that he was, indeed, their specialist!

The four men labored as one to make Johns Hopkins the best medical university in the world. Each was given *carte blanche* to develop his own department. Kelly spoke to the other three men about spiritual matters, but none of them responded.

In moving to Maryland to work at Johns Hopkins, Kelly had to relinquish his last ties to his clinic in Kensington. By 1892, he had opened the Howard A. Kelly Hospital in Baltimore and spent his time between it and his extensive duties at Johns Hopkins.

As a professor and practitioner in a leading university, Kelly exerted enormous influence. He gave his resident students the kind of responsibility he had always wanted; consequently, they were among the most able doctors of the day, sought for throughout America. They called him "chief" and spoke of him with veneration.

Kelly wrote extensively. In addition to two texts on gynecology, each the standard in its day, he compiled two dictionaries of medical biography, wrote a full-length life of **Walter Reed**, produced a colorful book on the snakes of Maryland, prepared a collection of biographies of American naturalists, and wrote an apologetic, *A Scientific Man and the Bible.*

A recurrent theme in Kelley's apologetic was his insistence that the Scriptures are utterly reliable. To attack them is to attack the foundation of faith. The gospel of John was a favorite target of the liberals. Yet the book of John, so warming to Kelly's soul, had within it such a simplicity of rich truths so in harmony with the rest of Scripture that Kelly found it impossible to believe it to be fraudulent. He learned Greek and Hebrew so that he could read the Bible in its original languages. He concluded, "Had we been a little wiser at the time in following more closely the work of the archaeologist in Egypt, in Asia Minor, in Palestine, and farther east, we might have noticed that the spades of the excavators from Layard and Rawlinson down through the decades were rapidly bringing data to the surface to prove irrefutably the accuracy of biblical narratives."

Few private libraries were more notable than Kelly's. It consisted of thousands of books. He gave many of these treasures away as soon as he was done with them. In addition, he produced a stereo clinic, in which he filmed operations by the greatest surgeons of the day. The series ran to eighty-four lessons. As well as all this, he often helped colleagues and students get their own works printed. He brought Max Broedel over from Germany, and together they created a new kind of medical drawing that students and colleagues found invaluable as an aid to their practice.

Kelly's faith taught him to do good to all people as opportunities arose. He was able to command high fees from his wealthy patients, and he invested these wisely. With his growing wealth, he supported his charity work. He endowed a fund to help indigent medical students; gave liberally to **Ida Scudder's** work in Vellore, India; and sponsored a boy's camp. He attempted to rescue women from prostitution and hired a nurse to run a home for women who had abandoned the streets for a decent life. He was active in politics, especially the temperance movement. While serving as a poll watcher, he was once assaulted. Explaining his continual involvement in good causes, he said, "There is no way to invest a life except in the lives of others."

His love of nature (and of snakes) never waned. He also loved astronomy. Unselfishly, he gave his favorite telescope to a class where the most students possible could use it. Every year, he explored a new river by canoe, often tackling dangerous rapids. In the wilds, a cottonmouth bit him on his small finger. Quickly, he applied a tourniquet, sucked out the poison, and became only mildly sick.

Kelly was a pioneer in the radium treatment of cancer. Doctors viciously attacked him as a quack for his experimental work with this radioactive substance. This attitude hurt Kelly deeply; nonetheless, he continued his work, which proved highly effective. He was vindicated a few years later when the same doctors who had attacked him gave him a standing ovation at a conference.

Good humor has been the saving of many a man, and Kelly was full of jokes. Once he dived to the bottom of a pool. Underwater a long time, he reemerged, to the awe of his students, with a live bass in his hand. They could not know that he had tethered it beforehand.

Not so funny was another dive. He struck bottom, smashed his shoulder, and narrowly missed breaking his neck. He suffered painful aftereffects for the rest of his life.

So full was Kelly's life that it is impossible to recount here all the good he did, the time he spent with his children, his love of his mother, the textbooks he wrote, the lives he reclaimed, his pulpit ministry as a layman, the Sunday school classes he taught, the students he set up in life, or the lasting friendships he formed. Perhaps it is sufficient to say that he was just nineteen when he arranged for the first boys' camp in America at Loyal Sock, a resort where he had himself found great enjoyment.

Kelly operated with a steady hand until he was eighty. Then the strain of operations became too great for him. The youngest of the Johns Hopkins four died in 1943 at age eighty-five. His wife died the same day.

The great doctor accomplished as much as he did because he yielded his life to the Lord. "God needs three talents," he said, "a will given over to Him, willing service, and persistence in service in spite of failure."

Wilfred Grenfell

(1865–1940)

Physician to Fishermen

Follow me and I will make you fishers of men.
(Matthew 4:19)

Not all doctors are famous for medical discoveries. Wilfred Grenfell, who boasted Viking ancestry, represents the doctor as adventurer. His active work among deep-sea fishermen won him international fame. He found the brave, hardworking folk of the Labrador and Newfoundland coasts with little in the way of spiritual guidance or medical succor, and founded a system that attended to both needs.

To follow Jesus Christ—I believe more than ever—that is the only real adventure of life," wrote Wilfred Grenfell. His was indeed an adventurous life.

"The child is father of the man," wrote William Wordsworth. It was well that Mrs. Grenfell let her son Wilfred run nearly unchecked. Undue restraint would not have prepared his body for the adventurous ministry the Lord planned for him. Energetic, he cared little for studies (although he learned readily enough when he chose). He would rather explore the Cheshire coast and the sands of Dee, leaping the dunes, climbing crags, or throwing himself into a strong undertow to experience the thrill of besting the elements.

Wilfred learned to shoot at a young age. One cold day when he was eight, he splashed into what he thought was a shallow puddle to retrieve a bit of game, found himself in a deep hole, and lost his gun in the scramble to save his life. He mourned the loss of the gun more than the soaking. Not until he was twelve was he again allowed to shoot alone, and even then, whether the weather was warm or freezing, he plunged into creek or sea to retrieve the game he brought down.

Wilfred idolized the tough fishermen who disembarked below the school. Although his father was a classical scholar and the local schoolmaster, Wilfred was as much at ease with the sturdy seamen as in his own refined home. The fishermen, in turn, welcomed him aboard their boats and allowed him to take their tillers as he adventured with them on the coastal waters. Sometimes he remained at sea with them all night. Wilfred and his brother, Algernon, built their own wobbly boat, which immediately capsized.

At fourteen, Wilfred's freedom was abruptly curtailed when he was packed off to boarding school. He was not happy. Needless to say, he was one of the boys who sneaked over the walls at night. Then he discovered sports, and suddenly life held renewed interest as he competed for glory. He played with verve. Throughout his life he hated to lose at anything.

When Wilfred was in his early teens, his father decided that he must put faith into action. He moved to the poverty-stricken east end of London to serve as a hospital chaplain with the city poor. Again, the Lord was planting influences. Not only did Wilfred see his father's faith in action but also London life taught Wilfred to hate alcohol, for he saw the misery it produced among poor Londoners.

Wilfred had given no thought to a career. When his father pointed out that he must soon decide what he would do with his life, the young man immediately announced that he would be a big game hunter. Hunting was unlikely to feed and clothe him, his father reminded him. He needed a *useful* career. Characteristically, Wilfred's decision to become a doctor was the impulse of a moment. He saw a brain pickled in a jar, realized the body was a mechanism that could be studied, and knew medicine was the science for him. At eighteen, he entered London Hospital Medical School.

Class work was a bore. And so Wilfred paid a bursar to mark him present when he was not. Sports was what fascinated him. He gathered athletes around him, hardened his body with exercise, and pressed himself to his limit with escapades such as swimming in ice-filled ponds.

Of course, he still had to pass exams. Cramming at the last minute, he managed it. Not until he began work in surgery did he give real attention to his studies. Under the fierce discipline of Frederick Treves (1853–1923), one of the ablest surgeons of the day, Wilfred learned doctoring. Treves became his youthful hero as the fishermen had been his childhood heroes and as Jesus Christ would be the hero of his mature age.

Evangelist Dwight L. Moody visited England, urging young men to turn to Christ. Wilfred dropped in on one of the tent meetings and committed himself. In another meeting two years later, Wilfred heard the Christian athlete C. T. Studd ask every person to stand who was on Christ's side. Among a group of boys from a reformatory ship, one rose, despite the hazing he knew he must take from his fellows. Grenfell was so impressed by this act of personal courage that he rose, too. That marked a turning point in his dedication to Christ.

At once, Grenfell began a work with slum lads, operating out of a Sunday school class he was asked to teach. He brought in the riffraff of the streets and built up their strength and fortitude, teaching them to row, lift weights—and box. This last activity was just too much for the stodgy pew warmers. The church asked him to leave. Wilfred said that this holier-than-thou attitude of churchgoers was the principle reason churches were failing to reach the world. He found new quarters, and his work paid off. Many of his boys became Christians and grew to be useful men. Some of them remained his close friends until death. This slum work initiated Grenfell into evangelization.

He went from the slums to the North Sea. At that time, North Sea fishing was a hard and hazardous enterprise that destroyed many lives each year. A man injured at sea was sent home with the catch of fish. He might toss for days in a small boat, broken limbs receiving further damage. Had there been a doctor in the fleet, much unnecessary suffering and the ruination of many lives could have been averted.

Another kind of ruin also lurked in wait for the fishermen. They had little to relieve their boredom, and wicked traders took advantage of this fact. Ships called "Copers" brought drink, tobacco, and pornography to the sailors, fleecing them of their hard-earned pay and corrupting their morals. A group of concerned citizens determined to change this. They founded the Royal National Mission to Deep-Sea Fishermen and acquired a boat to sell tobacco for half-price to the men as well as offering music, decent literature, and gospel influences as a substitute for the corruption brokered by the Copers. Treves, who spent a winter with the fishermen, urged Wilfred to become their doctor. Without hesitation, Wilfred agreed. This was the adventure he had always wanted.

Wilfred had found his milieu. He yarned with the men, invented games for them, toiled over the catch beside them, preached on their decks with simple parables drawn from everyday life. In this way, he won many of them to Christ. Able to outwork the best of the fishermen, Wilfred won their admiration. In turn, his hero-worship of them only grew. And his medical skill mended their bodies when they broke.

Grenfell's work was a success. The fishermen saw that he lived his faith and many wanted to become like him. His name became well known in Britain. Full of energy and faith, he always saw new ways to extend the work. His exuberance led to difficulties with the mission. For example, he committed them to building a shoreside clubhouse before they were ready. It was sorely needed. As soon as the fishermen hit port, they were under great pressure to squander their hard-earned gains on drink and other pleasures, to the neglect of their families. Grenfell wanted to provide an alternative. But the money wasn't there. To help raise it, Grenfell spoke wherever he could obtain an audience. His stories won people to open their pockets to the work and lift their prayers for the fishermen. For five years, Grenfell continued his work among the North Sea fishermen.

Those five years were the preface to a greater work that began in 1892. Lord Southborough, returning from a visit to Canada, asked the mission to investigate conditions in Labrador, which also depended upon fisheries for its livelihood. Grenfell was not just willing; he was eager.

The *Albert,* a small ship manned by seven crewmen and a captain, was outfitted, and Grenfell sailed as their doctor. St. Johns, Newfoundland, gave him a warm welcome; the city was in flames when he arrived. Despite their tragedy, the citizens greeted him joyously. He was urged to sail north to join the fishing fleet. The *Albert* picked its way four hundred miles up a badly charted coast to a cheerful welcome from the fleet. The doctor soon found medical work enough. Within two months, he had treated almost a thousand patients.

Conditions in Labrador were appalling. Poverty, ignorance, semistarvation, and tuberculosis were rife. A barter economy left the settlers at the mercy of traders. The Scotch and English settlers bore their hard lot with cheerful fortitude, but spiritual life was low despite the labors of Church of England parsons and Moravian and Methodist missionaries.

Grenfell recognized that one little hospital ship was inadequate to meet the needs of Labrador and Newfoundland. He vowed to find a way to provide clothes, medicine, and education. Christianity could make the difference. He urged the mission to open and support a work. Although fearing overextension and suspecting that Wilfred's enthusiasm would push them further and faster than they wanted to go, the directors agreed. Thus, in 1893, the operation that would become known as the Labrador Medical Mission was born.

In 1893, Grenfell made a heroic coast-hugging journey of over six hundred miles through largely uncharted waters, treating two thousand patients, including an Eskimo girl whose life he saved with an emergency operation. He convinced the fishermen around St. Anthony to relinquish their personal ambitions and donate their time to building themselves a hospital, which the mission would staff. They agreed. Grenfell was a firm believer in such cooperative action. His physical exploits, his vibrant faith, and his love won men and women to believe that they could undertake big things for themselves and their neighbors. In due course, Grenfell's vision was rewarded. Seven nursing stations, six permanent hospitals, a seaman's institute, four hospital ships, and several industrial centers, schools, food cooperatives, and clothing distribution centers came into existence.

The man seemed larger than life. His derring-do, impulsive gestures, and imperviousness to the cold, became legendary. So did the account of his marriage proposal. Traveling on the *Mauretania,* he fell in love with a wealthy girl "because of the way she walked." Through an error in the passenger list, he supposed that she was someone other than who she was. Boldly, he reproved her for the frivolous life she was leading.

"But you don't even know my name," she retorted.

Adroitly countering this punch, Grenfell replied that what her name *was* did not matter. He was only interested in what he hoped it was *going* to be. The upshot was that Anne MacClanahan married him.

The Labradorians once thought that they had lost Grenfell. A seal hunter spotted small figures drifting on ice two miles from shore. Within hours, pounding feet brought the news down the coast: Wilfred Grenfell was marooned on an ice pan with his sled dogs. Against all advice, the doctor had raced off to tend a sick boy. That was Grenfell's way. When work was waiting, there was no time to waste. Let others dither and cavil. With his exuberance and energy, he would conquer all obstacles.

At the mission hospital, everyone spoke in hushed voices. If the doctor died, their work was doomed. More than anyone else, he had been Labrador's champion. At times, it seemed as though Grenfell *was* the mission. Since 1893, he had raised most of the Labrador Mission's support through speaking tours, book writing, and the formation of associations. More than his life, his very work was jeopardized by his foolhardy venture onto the bay in such weather.

With night approaching, the men could do nothing except dig up a boat, buried by winter snow and ice, and get ready to attempt a rescue as soon as light permitted—if there was anyone left to rescue. The wind was pushing the pans out to sea. Once past the headland, Grenfell's ice raft would break up. The cold might kill him long before that. The night seemed an eternal wait.

Dawn came at last. "He's there!" someone shouted. Far to windward, but still within the shelter of the bay, they sighted the doctor through the telescope, still moving. Heedless of their own safety, five brave men launched the boat and paddled into the grinding ice to rescue the man who had dedicated his life to bringing them medicine and the gospel. They knew that what they were doing was incredibly dangerous.

Five, ten, a dozen times they had to leap from their boat onto ice pans and haul it up to prevent it being crushed. Steadily, they worked their way through soft sish (wind-packed snow) toward the stranded evangelist. At last, they could make out his features. His face was a weird red. He was clad in dog skins. As they came alongside, no joke dropped from his mouth. He scrambled silently into the boat with his animals. The crew poured him tea and, turning into the wind, strained for shore.

At last, Grenfell spoke. Over and over he apologized for the trouble he'd caused. He told how he had attempted to take a short cut, how his sled had sunk into sish, how he had slashed the traces so the dogs wouldn't perish, and how all of them had swum to the nearest ice pan. It had been a small pan, and he'd had to coax the dogs back into the water to swim to a larger pan twenty yards away. To save his life, he'd been forced to kill two of his faithful dogs and dress himself in their skins, for his clothes were waterlogged, and he would soon have frozen. Indeed, his feet *were* frozen; the pain of returning circulation testified to that.

Grenfell survived this desperate adventure to continue his labors in Newfoundland and Labrador until ill health forced him to retire in 1935. His once-robust mind began to fail. By then, the mission had become self-perpetuating. His successes were made possible by thousands of individuals in the English-speaking world who contributed time, money, prayer, and clothes. Christian doctors and nurses volunteered for the wastes of Labrador and staffed the hospitals he built.

26

Ida Scudder

(1870–1960)

Founder of Vellore Christian Medical College

Clothe yourselves with compassion. (Colossians 3:12)

Ida S. Scudder represents the doctor as founder of a foreign medical school to pass on the West's hard-won medical knowledge to a people suffering under an archaic tradition. Doctors have long realized the need to train successors to carry on their work. Christians, too, have been prominent in this work. Ida was not the first doctor to see the need for training medical personnel in India, but she may have been the boldest and most successful.

Colonel Bryson of the British Medical Department of Madras was incredulous. "It would be ridiculous if it wasn't so—so heroic!" he exclaimed. Sitting across from him was Ida Scudder. To her there was nothing heroic about starting a desperately needed school to train nurses—even if she had no buildings, no money, no staff. Rooms could be rented. Money was even now being raised. As for staff, *she* could teach, couldn't she?

"You'll be lucky if you get three applicants," growled the Colonel. Didn't she realize that this was *India,* where women were held in near-total subjugation and assumed to have no brains of their own? "If you get as many as six, go ahead and start your school. You have government permission." Ida's heart beat with joy as she left. She knew the applicants would be there.

Beautiful and vivacious, Ida Scudder had not always dreamed of building a medical school for Indian women. Instead, she fantasized about marrying a millionaire and enjoying the good life. In her mind, the good life was to live in America, far from India where she had been raised by her missionary-doctor father. It was a hot, overcrowded land that was subject to drought, famine, and plague, and alien in its religious thinking.

Her dream was changed by a succession of events. In 1890, Ida was in the United States attending school at Dwight L. Moody's seminary for girls. Word reached her that her mother was ill. She was needed to tend the family in India. Dutifully, she abandoned her madcap escapades—sneaking down fire escapes for unchaperoned visits to town, "borrowing" the German instructor's horse and carriage for an unpremeditated ride and tying it up two miles away, protesting seminary food, and smoking in the attic—and rejoined her parents. All the same, she promised herself that some day she would escape India for good. As a child, she had broken bread to feed to children too weak from famine to feed themselves. She had seen their corpses lying beside the road. Happy would be the day when she could thrust such scenes and memories from her!

It took the sufferings of three young girls to change her mind. One night as she sat in her room, a high-caste Brahmin stepped onto the veranda and asked her to come attend his child-wife, who was in labor. The barber women had done all they could. Without help, the girl would die. Ida knew nothing about midwifery, she said, but her father was a skilled doctor; when he returned, she would bring him.

The Brahmin refused. "She had better die than have a man come into the house," he said and left. Thinking of the desperate girl, too young to bear a baby, Ida was moved.

Again footsteps sounded on the veranda. Perhaps the Brahmin had relented? Ida ran down. Instead, she saw that a Muslim had come to her. "Please come help my wife," he pleaded. She was dying in labor. Ida knew no more obstetrics than she had an hour earlier. John Scudder offered to go in her place, but the Muslim refused. No man outside his family had ever looked on his wife's face. He could not let a foreign male approach her. Ida and John were unable to change his mind. Ida returned to her room and picked up a book to distract herself but found that she could take no interest in it.

Again she heard footsteps. Perhaps the Muslim was back? Again she ran down. To her horror, yet a third man appeared, a high-caste Hindu. He, too, had a young wife dying in labor. Would Ida come? He, too, refused the help of John Scudder. Only a woman could tend his wife.

> "I could not sleep that night—it was too terrible," wrote Ida later. "Within the very touch of my hand were three young girls dying because there was no woman to help them. I spent much of the night in anguish and prayer. I did not want to spend my life in India. My friends were begging me to return to the joyous opportunities of a young girl in America, and somehow I felt I could not give that up. I went to bed in the early morning after praying much for guidance. I think that was the first time I ever met God face to face, and all that time it seemed that He was calling me into this work.
>
> Early in the morning I heard the 'tom-tom' beating in the village and it struck terror in my heart, for it was a death message. I sent our servant, who had come up early, to the village to find out the fate of these three women, and he

came back saying that all of them had died during the night. . . . Again I shut myself in my room and thought very seriously about the condition of the Indian women and, after much thought and prayer, I went to my father and mother and told them that I must go home and study medicine, and come back to India to help such women."

Ida was fortunate that other women such as as Elizabeth Blackwell had already forced a passage through medical school. Because of them, she was able to attend medical classes in Philadelphia and at Cornell. Furthermore, the work of **Clara Swain**, the first woman missionary doctor, had shown that women doctors could be effective in India.

Tropical medicine was not taught at Ida's schools, but she read what she could. She learned that the Indians in an 1896 outbreak of the black plague refused vaccination, believing the shots were given to poison them. Ida realized that she would be facing deadly superstition and fear when she returned to India.

She almost did not live to return. On a bicycle tour to address missionary meetings, Ida became infected from contaminated well water. Her life teetered in grave danger. Fortunately, a famous doctor was able personally to supervise her case. His care, the strength of her body, and the prayers of friends such as evangelist Dwight L. Moody saved her life.

Dr. Louise Hart, who had worked with John Scudder at both Ranipet and Vellore, also saw the need of India's women. She now wrote to Ida, asking her to raise fifty thousand dollars for a women's hospital at Vellore, a sum equivalent to at least five hundred thousand dollars today. Ida began to canvass for the money, but mission authorities, doubting so large a sum could be raised, told her she might request only eight thousand dollars. Ida thought they were wrong. If the money was needed, God would provide it. However, she obeyed. Dollars trickled in, "an ounce of water to quench an elephant's thirst." She was to sail for India in a week, so she rushed to see anyone she thought might be able to help. One person to whom she presented her case was Miss Harriet Taber, president of a missionary society.

Ida poured out her heart to Miss Taber, telling her of India's need and her own call to the work. Miss Taber arranged for her to speak to a women's society the following Monday. On Sunday morning, Ida received a note asking her to call Monday on Mr. Schell, the president of a New York bank. Schell was the elderly brother-in-law of Miss Taber and had met Ida at his sister-in-law's house the evening before. Little help was expected from him as he was reputed to be a tightwad, but Ida paid the call anyhow. Unknown to her, Schell had overheard her entire impassioned plea.

He grilled Ida with questions about her proposed work. "And what makes you think that you, a mere girl, can run a hospital?" he asked.

Ida replied that she would be working beside her father, an experienced doctor. Satisfied at last, Schell turned and wrote a check. Name the hospital for his late wife, Mary Taber Schell, he said. When Ida saw the size of the check, she could hardly contain her delight. It was for ten thousand dollars! This evidence of God's power led her to reprove the board that had held her back. "Now there, *there* would have been my fifty thousand dollars if you had not stopped me!" she exclaimed.

As it turned out, she did not work long beside her father. He died shortly after she returned to India. She had to undertake the enterprise on her own. With no facilities—the Mary Taber Schell Women's Hospital could not be built for two years—she turned an eight-by-twelve-foot room into her dispensary. The veranda would serve as a waiting room.

Not that she was seeing patients. Suspicion and doubt kept the Tamil Indians from approaching her. When she did finally receive a call, it was to a desperate case for which she could do nothing. Word spread that her first patient had died. Suspicion increased. But God had not equipped her so thoroughly to leave her idle very long.

Eventually, a high-caste Hindu woman ventured to have her eyes examined. She had dangerous conjunctivitis. Ida was successful in treating the case. Demands for her services increased steadily after that. Soon, she was seeing one hundred, two hundred, three hundred, even five hundred cases a day. In desperation, Ida had to conscript her very willing kitchen maid to help her. Salomi was the first of many nurses Ida would train.

India's need was desperate. There was but one doctor for every ten thousand people. Traditional practitioners had a few excellent remedies but more that were dangerously harmful. For example, a "doctor" might treat an eye disease with a concoction of ground pepper and glass. Ida's compassion revolted at this quackery. Compassion drove her to take on more and more work. The pressure was tremendous. Sometimes she exclaimed, "Oh for the quiet order of a well-run insane asylum!" She began to carry her services to the countryside villages, first by oxcart and then by car. Villagers gathered along the roadsides, waiting for her. As she drove home exhausted at night, men and women would flag her down to tend some desperate case. Few of these people could pay.

The need was desperate, and she was but one woman. True, Dr. Anne Kugler was opening a Lutheran school to train nurses, but what was that in contrast to the need? Even if dozens more doctors came from America and Europe, their services would be like a drop of water in the ocean. Indian women must be taught to care for Indian women. That idea was the germ for the Vellore medical school. Once it was opened, Ida set her sights higher. If she could train nurses, she could train doctors.

On March 24, 1922, her first class of women doctors graduated. Condescending officials said her graduates could never compete with the men in the national exams. She'd be lucky to see a single woman pass, they said. Ida vowed to get at least one woman through. As the results of the first exam were announced, her stress mounted. The men were announced first. Only 20 percent of them passed. The tests were very hard. If only one woman might pass! The results came, and Ida could shout with joy. Inspired by her genius and vision, *all* of Ida's students passed! One official remarked wryly that it seemed as if India's women would set too high a standard for the men!

None of this achievement came easily. Ida did the work of six people. Backers such as Gertrude Dodd, Hilda Olsen, and Lucy Peabody struggled long and hard during the Great Depression and World War II to raise funds to support the Vellore project as it grew. Time after time the Lord brought the work to the very brink of crisis before rescuing it. One rescue came through a donation given at the last minute. Another time, the work was saved by the extension of a deadline. On still another occasion, salvation was through Ida's willingness to change her vision and include men in the college. Once, when Ida was almost ready to give up on her hope of a college for doctors, one of her students shared an encouraging word with her that steeled Ida to go forward. She went into her room and wrote, "First ponder, then dare. Know your facts. Count the cost. Money is not the most important thing. What you are building is not a medical school. It is the kingdom of God. Don't err on the side of being too small. If this is the will of God that we should keep the college open, *it has to be done*."

Through it all, Vellore survived to provide a base for the work of several great Christian doctors, among them Jessie Findlay, Carol Jameson, Flora Innes, Dr. Cochrane, **Paul Brand**, Pauline Jeffery, Hilda Lazarus, and Ida B. Scudder, a niece. Ida had a way of charging others with her vision. Dr. Reeve Betts gave up a lucrative practice in Boston to head the department of thoracic surgery. Dr. John Gault came from Australia to become the pathologist. To name these few is to ignore many more. Increasingly, however, the names were Indian. One of her best students, Miriam Manuel, refused a high-paying position in order to stay on as Vellore's professor of obstetrics. Another of her students, Dr. Kamala Vythilingham, became the school's cardiologist. Through them, Ida's vision was being fulfilled. Indian women were caring for Indian women!

In four generations, Ida Scudder's family sent forty-two missionaries to India and other nations. Irrepressible Ida, full of energy and vitality, was perhaps the greatest of them all, and the Indians sensed it. Many of them knelt before her, believing her to be the incarnation of some god.

The aura of Ida's greatness emanated out of her ability to rise to any challenge. For example, when Ida was sixty-five, she drew the teen champion in a Ladies Recreation Club tennis tournament. "I've drawn a grannie," wailed the girl.

"I'll teach her to 'grannie' me!" exclaimed Ida, and she played so fiercely that the girl did not win a single game in their two sets.

Ida's strength was in Christ. She not only used her surgeon fingers as His witness but also taught through Bible lessons and speeches. The Bible lessons continue; Vellore Christian Medical College gives ten lessons a day. Ida's focus is best summarized in commencement remarks she gave to her first, triumphant graduating class: "And last and greatest of all, may you follow always and closely in the footsteps of the Great Physician, Christ, who went about doing good, healing the sick, outpouring His wealth of love upon a sinning, sorrowing world, encouraging, uplifting, and carrying joy wherever He went."

27

John Flynn

(1880–1951)

Founder of the Aerial Medical Service

*Each of you should look not only to your own interests,
but also to the interests of others. (Philippians 2:4)*

Strictly speaking, John Flynn does not belong in this
book. He was not a doctor. Beyond the use of first aid (on
which he prepared a handbook), he did not practice
medicine. And yet he cannot be excluded. John Flynn was
so interested in medical problems and so instrumental
in solving them that great libraries classify his biography
with eminent physicians. John Flynn is an example of a
leader who brought twentieth-century innovations—
some developed at his own behest—to the service of
medicine.

The outback. Vast and beautiful, but often treacherous and deso-
late, it dominates the interior of Australia. Although gritty ex-
plorers early gave their lives to map its vast reaches, much of it remains uninhabited to this day, the domain of gibber (stony desert) and
sand ridges. The majority of Australians live along green coastal strips
of land, especially those that lie east of the Great Dividing Range,
where the watershed brings short rivers down to the Pacific and rain-
fall rises above twenty inches a year. The same was true a century ago.
When John Flynn was born in 1880, virtually all of Australia's two
million inhabitants lived on less than a quarter of the Continent.

Just a handful of people—mere thousands of white people and
not many more aborigines—inhabited the remaining three-quarters
of the continent. Much of Australia's history and literature and song
exalts those few, glorifying their heroism. Most of them were men.
By and large, the outback wasn't much of a place to bring a woman
at the beginning of the twentieth century. Throughout its immensity,
there were few midwives and precious little water in which to wash
diapers. The loneliness, the lack of medical care, and the scarcity of
amenities could produce real hardship, especially for pregnant women
and for mothers. What woman wants to drudge alone in the blazing
heat while her man is away for days and weeks with his mates, riding
muster on cattle? Consequently, for every woman in the outback,
there were ten men.

Sheep and cattle ranches and gold, opal, and wolfram mines were
the main industries—especially sheep and cattle. To support live-
stock on the semi-arid hills and plateaus of northern and western
Australia, ranch spreads had to be vast. The distance between homes
was in many regions measured in miles, sometimes tens of miles,
sometimes a hundred or more. A person receiving serious injury in a
remote region would have to be transported hundreds of miles by
primitive conveyance over unpaved tracks to the nearest medical
facility for treatment. Often enough, the nearest medical help was in
a city that hugged the coast. More than any other individual, John
Flynn changed that state of affairs.

Like most Australians, John grew up in the east. He was born at
Moliagul in Victoria, a town northwest of Melbourne that does not

appear on many maps. His father was a school teacher and a lay
pastor in the Methodist church. John had little recollection of his
beautiful and gracious mother, for she died when he was three. For a
year after his mother's death, relatives cared for John, but after his
father transferred to a school near Melbourne, John was able to re-
join him. The only church near their new home was Presbyterian.
That became the denomination in which John was raised and through
which he did his work.

Shy and self-effacing, he became a school teacher. He was described as one of the "most trustworthy, painstaking and upright
pupils" at the University of Melbourne. He was all of that as a teacher,
too. It wasn't enough for him to *teach* his pupils. He must learn
about them, about their families, their lives. He could never just re-
buke a student for falling asleep in class. He had to know *why.* And
so he visited the parents in the evenings and talked with them and
shared their chores. He learned to milk cows, the same cows that his
students rose at 4:00 A.M. to milk before they came to school so tired
they couldn't keep their eyes open.

He taught himself to shoot and cycled over the country with a
rifle slung on his shoulder. Shocked by the lack of religious education in his district, he opened a Sunday school to bring light to souls.

So many souls. His heart began to pull toward the ministry. That
he did not rush into the pulpit was owing to a couple factors. For
one, he wasn't sure that was what *God* wanted of him. You don't just
thrust yourself into the ministry. For another thing, he was not sure
where he'd find money to attend seminary. Yet there was no mistak-
ing the trend of his thought expressed in a letter to his father.

> If Jesus of Nazareth be indeed the Son of Almighty God; if
> He was in reality "God with us" showing us the Father; if it
> is a fact that we only sojourn on this earth for a little while,
> and then appear before the creator of the universe; if it be
> really true that the Power who made us desires us to live in
> constant communion with Him, well, why are these truths
> not more responded to than they are? If it is true that Jesus
> is God's Son, and that through Him whosoever-will may

approach the Father Himself, what more honorable calling
can a man follow than to realize this fact and act upon it?

John was a plugger. Over a period of several years, while teaching in various places, he took his seminary training. Meanwhile, he
acquired experience by working with youths in the slums of
Melbourne. Photography interested him. He made himself an expert. First aid seemed useful. He made himself an expert.

No one could grow up in Australia without hearing heroic stories
of the outback. An account of shipwreck and bare survival drew
John's attention to that vast wilderness. He'd like to have a go at
some work there, he decided.

Perhaps he wanted to test his mettle. Perhaps he wanted to feel
from inside what it was to be part of the fabric that made up Australia's
legend and heroic history, that made Henry Lawson's outback tales
live. He participated in mission work to shearers, including an adventurous camel trek across the desert. Twice he went out West. It
wasn't enough to teach. He had to ask questions. His eyes were
opened. He saw the beauty of shifting sands and star-decked nights.
He learned labor and solitude. He learned the need.

Lacking pastors, bushmen did not even have a burial service to
say over a dead mate. Few of them had any good idea how to handle
the medical crises that so often arose in that harsh land. A handbook
was needed to bring together essential first aid and spiritual knowledge for bushmen. John compiled the *Bushman's Companion,* got
the mission to print thousands of copies, and saw that they were
distributed. When God shows you a need, you've got to do something about it. All of these activities were first steps toward a life's
work. God is not hasty. Neither was John.

In 1911, at age thirty-one, John volunteered for a parish that
stretched from the Flinder's Range in South Australia to Oodnadatta
deep in the Great Victoria Desert. The Presbyterian church had placed
a trained nurse at Oodnadatta, providing a modicum of medical assistance to a wide, neglected region. With John's efforts to fund and
build a hospital for her and his treks to lonely outposts to preach the
gospel, his work truly began.

It became a vision, even an obsession with him. More than most, he saw clearly the potential of the outback and its desperate cry for essential services: rapid communication, quicker medical attention, and spiritual training. What could one man do? Ride from station to station, talk to a few people, and ride on. He did that for the Smith of Dunesk Mission. It wasn't enough. What was needed were thousands of people sharing the same vision. Well, he could issue a magazine. He knew how to write. School teachers do that kind of thing. He knew how to take pictures. He had learned photography. He would tell people about the outback—show them the potential of the outback—and get thousands working with him.

So John founded a magazine called the *Inlander,* a magazine to promote tirelessly his dream of supplying pastors and roads and railroads and nurses for the outback. He filled the magazine with photographs and charts so that people could visualize what he was saying. "We can station padres and nurses at a dozen key points," said John, "and provide a blanket of security for the whole outback."

A man with that kind of vision cannot be suppressed indefinitely. The board saw that he was the right man for the job and made him director of the Australian Inland Mission. That was in 1912. He preached his vision of outback development to all who would listen. At his instigation, committees were formed in towns to raise money for the work. Money was scarce and hurdles were enormous. Disinterested officials had to be persuaded, conflicting state interests resolved, the medical community involved, the bushmen won from their instinctive distrust of anything that smelled like a handout. Only a patient man could get over hurdles like that and show that every hand that could be signed up was indispensable. John was patient because his God was patient. Bit by bit, he won his victories. One victory came when two bushmen who were the chief opponents of a nursing hostel at Alice Springs became the station's first patients and afterwards its most vocal supporters.

Year after year, John lobbied, educated, and pleaded. He pleaded not only for ministerial and nursing stations strategically placed throughout the outback but also for radio communications between the settlers and the outside world and for vehicles to transport the sick to the coast for care. Books were needed, too. Many men had nothing to read but the labels on soup cans.

Tragedies highlighted the need for these essential services. In one particularly heartrending case, a young man had to be operated on without anesthetic by inadequately trained personnel, obeying instructions relayed by Morse code on radios that Flynn provided. The operation lasted seven hours, and a postmortem examination showed that it was well done, but all of the agony was in vain. Within a month, the man died from complications. Had better transportation or a skilled doctor been available, he would have lived.

Piece by piece, John's vision was fulfilled. Port Hedland got its hospital in 1915, Marandy in 1917, Halls Creek in 1918, Beltana in 1919 . . . and so it went. Rail lines were built, easing the outback's isolation. Padres were positioned to patrol huge tracts of wilderness with the gospel. Funds trickled in for nursing stations, and by 1923, twenty of them had been opened. Brave and hardy women, such as Sisters E. A. Mains and M. A. Latto Bett, did much to uplift the tone of life in the outback, for their hospitals and hostels became the center of social life in the community. Men cleaned up their behavior and washed their bodies before approaching the ministering women.

John was quick to see the potential of the airplane. If doctors could fly to patients . . . He called for the acquisition of planes and the provision of flying doctors at strategic locations. Again he had an uphill push, but he knew how to persist because his God was also persistent. After many years, patience won. The world's first flying doctor service, not reliant on military planes, came into being at Cloncurry, Queensland. They named it the Australian Inland Mission's Aerial Medical Service. Doctor K. St. Vincent Welch answered his first call on May 17, 1928. That call involved two minor surgeries.

Perhaps no case more vividly demonstrates the hardships of the outback and the worth of the flying doctor service than an incident at Broken Hill, over on the western side of New South Wales by Barrier Range. A manager's wife lapsed suddenly into a coma. Her husband rode twelve miles through torrential rain to reach the nearest radio set. There he succeeded in sending out a call for help. He was told to prepare an airstrip. Since the flat lands were under water, he had to clear a gravel ridge, which meant laboring all night, hacking down brush and over a hundred trees. In the morning he radioed again. The flying doctor was answering another emergency, but the manager was told to create dark smoke in about two hours as the plane should be able to get there by then and needed some guide in that featureless land. How should he make the smoke? asked the manager.

"Burn old tires," came the reply. He had no old tires, only the four on his car. Using horse harnesses, the manager and a couple of other men got the heavy woman up the hill.

At the specified time the exhausted manager lit the first tire. The plane did not appear. The smoke thinned. He lit a second tire. Still no plane. The third went up in smoke. No plane. Desperate, he lit the last tire. The plane appeared. Three months later, the wife was back, completely restored to health.

All of this was possible only because of breakthroughs in wireless radio. A cheap, compact radio that could work in the bush had been developed. Again, John was the spark. Alfred Traeger (1895–1980), a devout Lutheran and a technical genius, labored beside him. Many years of partly successful experiments resulted in the creation of a pedal set that most stations could afford and that could be used anywhere in the bush. Finally, women could break the isolation of their often grim lives. Many of them learned Morse code so they could "speak" to the outside. Thousands upon thousands of messages were relayed through Flynn's mission stations, some for medical attention, others for spiritual counsel, but most for business. Eventually, after Morse code gave way to voice-radio, outback children were even educated by radio, fulfilling another of John's dreams.

That John, the Presbyterian, worked so closely with Traeger, the Lutheran, illustrates another facet of his character. He was avowedly ecumenical. The task was too big for one denomination.

Such a decision demonstrated the depths of his insight. He often displayed such wisdom. To a frustrated doctor, whose every move was impeded by obstructions, he wrote, "Try to be swayed only by considerations of a permanent nature." To one of his supporters he wrote, "My own belief is that no man is sufficient for any task handed out to him, but that if he faces the task, the Great Father, day by day, supplies all rations as they become necessary. A man does not start out ready-made. He is the product of countless emergencies, bravely met and overcome—each of which leaves in his personality its own deposit of wisdom and power."

Flynn once remarked, "A man is his friends." All that he accomplished was possible because he wove an enormous web of friendships. Many of those friendships came about because he had a knack for getting others to share his vision. They wanted to be part of the future he saw. Other friendships were cemented in more down-to-earth ways. John was as handy as he was practical. Wherever he stayed, he fixed clocks, broken china, eggbeaters, and other small utensils, leaving behind him a residue of good will.

World War II brought great changes to the outback. Where pounds and shillings had trickled in before, the war effort brought millions. Roads were paved and airfields built. General Douglas MacArthur praised John's communication system, which greatly aided the Allies' initial efforts to establish forward bases.

The AIM Aerial Medical Service became the Royal Flying Doctor Service. To bushmen and their lonely wives, it did not matter what the service was called. The gift of medical facilities on the ground and from the air had thrown a mantle of security over their lives. John Flynn was the propelling force behind both. That is why he belongs in this book.

28

Arthur Rendle Short

(1880–1953)

The Surgeon Who Defended Christianity

Heaven and earth will pass away, but my words will never pass away. (Matthew 24:35)

Christian doctors, from St. Luke until today, have defended the faith. One thinks of S. I. McMillen, Thomas Willis, Paul Brand, Peter Mark Roget, William Keen, Howard Atwood Kelly, and Charles Bell. Rendle Short, when he is remembered, is remembered as an apologist, for he turned his keen intellect to well-written proofs of Christianity. He represents the doctor as defender of the faith.

Arthur Rendle Short was well equipped to speak with assurance on matters touching both faith and medical science. He wrote:

> It is not to be suspected on ordinary grounds that a small se-
> cluded nation like the Hebrews, lately come out of the desert,
> would have any better ideas of health and disease than were
> current amongst a great settled civilization like that of Egypt.
> It is the more surprising, therefore, to find in the Old Testa-
> ment the observations of disease so accurate, and the sanitary
> science so much in accord with modern knowledge. . . .
> Whence had the Biblical writer this insight, two or three thou-
> sand years in advance of his day? [A]ll these principles are so
> free from paganism or magic, are so simple, so scientific, so
> neglected for centuries only to be rediscovered within our
> own lifetime, so little likely to be due to the observation of a
> people as primitive as the Israelites, a thousand or fifteen hun-
> dred years before Christ, that we must surely conclude that
> the writers had a special revelation from God.

As a surgeon, Short had medical expertise. As a member of the despised Plymouth Brethren, he had known George Müller of Bristol, one of the best-known advocates of faith ministry. Müller's faith had been imparted to Rendle, who remembered the beloved old man laying his hands upon his boyish head, saying, "God bless you, my boy, and make you a blessing to others."

The association with Müller was more than casual. William Short, Rendle's grandfather, had taught in Müller's orphanages, trusting the Lord for the needs of the hour. Rendle's parents, following in that faith, were also dedicated to the reclamation of lost souls.

With such family influences and the living example of parents and grandparents continually before his eyes, it would seem there was little danger that Rendle would lapse into secularism or Dar-winism. However, as an intellectual among Christians who were not rigorous in their thinking, he craved reasonable grounds for his faith. This was the heady first era of the Darwinists and of German textual criticism, both of which attacked the Bible. Rendle had to know for himself what was true. "I could not follow cunningly devised fables, however glamorous," he wrote.

Fortunately for him, he fell in with an apologetic work by Henry Drummond that convinced him that "a synthesis between natural science and the Christian message was not impossible, and that the designer of the world might very well be the God of the Christian." His assurance that the New Testament was what it purported to be was increased when he read Doctor Hobart's old book *The Medical Language of St. Luke.* This work showed him that Luke and Acts, by their use of twenty-three technical medical terms not found in other New Testament books, proved that Luke was indeed a medical man, as Paul had said. The cumulation of such evidence gave him a fixed certainty that the Scriptures were authentic. As always, truth has implications. "[I]f the Christian has definitely come to the decision that the Bible is the word of God for him, what follows but that it becomes his unfailing guide, which must at all costs be obeyed?"

Rendle Short answered his own question by choosing obedience. A love of the natural sciences brought him into medicine. Once he determined to become a doctor, he also determined to become a medical missionary. It is, of course, not enough merely to *want* to be something for God. We must do our part to achieve the goal. Rendle applied himself so assiduously to his work that he took honors in every subject for which he ever sat. He even swept every scholarship available to him. Scholarships paid his entire education; he could not have afforded medical training otherwise. So successful was he at mopping up scholarships, the school changed the rules so that no other single student could ever again win all the prizes.

Rendle did something that made little sense to his classmates. He took classes in tropical medicine. His fellow students did not realize that he was preparing for his goal of becoming a missionary. With the same purpose in mind, he gave almost every free minute to Christian service.

Intense application and deep shyness combined in Rendle to give him a severe and gruff exterior, according to biographer William Capper. He was not readily able to put others at their ease. And yet he was able to enter any home, even of degenerate alcoholics, and kneel in prayer beside them. One man marveled after Rendle had knelt on the stone floor and prayed for him. "What do you think of a doctor like that, kneeling next to a man like me down here? If he knew what I was like, he wouldn't talk to me. Thank God for such men! It's the first prayer that has been prayed in this home." Short was God's means of reconciling another man to the wife who had left him because of constant foul language. The man began to attend Bible class and soon was reading Scripture with a child on his knee.

Although he could be brusque, Rendle was a bit of a prankster and humorist. As a practical joke, he heated the stools of the anatomy students as hot as he could get them to enjoy their surprise when they sat down. He corrected one student's spelling mistake with the wry comment, "*Vomitting* is only spelled with two t's in especially severe cases."

When Rendle became a full surgeon at thirty-three, he and his wife, Helen Case, sought to enter the mission field for which he had trained. Surprisingly, Rendle found himself blocked at every turn! He realized that the Lord intended him for work in England. He undertook that work with vigor, speaking regularly to groups about Christ, giving here a devotional and there a defense of faith in the living Lord. From his own early struggles to believe, he knew apologetics to be necessary, and he was eager to help others over the hurdles of faith.

The apostle Paul, noted Rendle, carried the gospel to the centers of trade, intellect, and industry in the Roman world. He sought to do the same. The center of ideas in the modern world is the university; therefore, he not only urged students to share the gospel with their classmates but also did his part. InterVarsity Fellowship found that they could count on him for any assistance that lay in his power. At various times, he served as president, vice-president, or treasurer of the organization. He organized many student ministries and conferences and taught a student Bible study in his own home.

Rendle Short always found time to speak of Christ and to assist Christ's workers. Missionaries found that his wallet was open to them. He not only treated them free of charge but also provided them with carefully selected medical tools. In such ways he extended his witness for his Lord.

Practical in the application of his faith, he worked with the Shaftesbury campaigns for the downtrodden and for Müller's orphanages. He was also a first-rate surgeon, much respected by his fellow physicians for his swift, bold, and decisive action. While no great medical discovery is attributed to him, he was an expert on appendicitis.

Rendle's witness lives on in the lives of those he touched. It lives on also in the careful apologetic works he wrote. He was not one to sugarcoat faith. "Christians are the *salt* of the earth, not its *sugar*," he remarked. The titles of his books show a willingness to confront tough intellectual challenges to Scripture with solid research: *The Historic Truth in the Light of Today, The Bible and Modern Research, Archaeology Gives Evidence, Why Believe, Modern Discovery and the Bible, In the Days of the Prophet Isaiah, The Bible and Modern Medicine,* and *Wonderfully Made.*

Every good apologist is Christ-centered because Christ is the essence of our faith. Rendle was no exception. Writing of our need for Christ, he said, "If someone says he has no such sense of need, the answer is simple; he has never had his eyes opened to the holiness of God, nor to the guilt of human sin. He is living in a fool's paradise, like a man with leprosy or cancer who does not know it. That sense of need makes us put our faith in Jesus Christ. . . ." Noting the differences in the ways people come to Christ, he wrote, "[T]he door of entrance may seem to us to be painted in differing colors, but it opens on to Christ himself, the Way, the Truth, and the Life."

Rendle spent much time in prayer and Bible reading. Did this make him self-righteous? Quite the contrary. It was probably with himself in mind that he wrote these words: "The nearer you are to light, the darker is your shadow. Thus the one who has the greater light is often the most conscious of wrong in himself."

29

Paul White

(1910–1992)

"Jungle Doctor" from Australia

He taught them many things by parables. (Mark 4:2)

Jesus taught in parables. Many of His followers have also found them to be an effective means of communicating the gospel. So did Paul White, who wove parables into his novels, *Jungle Doctor* books, fables, and autobiographical writings. Numerous doctors have produced literature. Paul White represents the doctor as author.

"G od seldom blows a trumpet when he is indicating a change in our lives," wrote Paul White in his autobiography, *Alias Jungle Doctor.* God's working is more commonly in the form of small seeds planted one day to sprout in the rains of another. He prepares us for change through impressions, seemingly casual influences, and small shifts of focus whose importance we do not recognize until later. Paul's life exemplifies this pattern.

One shift in thinking came to Paul as he spoke about repentance to a group of hospitalized Africans. Sighs of weariness rose from the edge of his audience. Dan Mbogoni, Paul's African assistant, touched his shoulder. "Stop now, Bwana. This is *mabulibuli du —* only smoke and steam. Do you really understand what you are trying to say?" Paul realized he did not. His dictionary and commentary soon showed him that "to repent" meant "to think again" or "to change one's mind."

Dan told him that the local Wagogo people had a way of making abstract ideas clear. Next day, Paul listened as Dan told a fable: For revenge, monkey went up a tree to chop off his uncle's favorite branch. Giraffe saw at once that monkey was on the wrong side of the cut and urged him to change his mind. Despite repeated warnings, monkey refused. Monkey, ax, and limb toppled together into a ravine.

The story chiseled a picture of repentance into the minds of the patients. Whether Dan knew it or not, he had made his point using the same technique as Christ, who used word pictures about coins and narrow gates and houses built on sand. The significance was not lost on Paul White. "My target now was to present the great facts of Christianity in a way that everybody could understand," he wrote later. On hot African evenings, he absorbed African tales. At that time, he had no idea of becoming a writer. His concern as a missionary doctor was to use the best available methods, whether healing bodies or illuminating souls. But a seed had been planted.

That Paul was in Tanganyika (modern Tanzania) in 1937 was owing to other seeds. His father, Richard White, served in the Boer war in Southern Africa. When he came home, he told his son fascinating tales of the Zulus and their country—tales that fired Paul's imagination and filled him with a longing to visit Africa. Richard

White died of meningitis in army camp in 1914. This meant a reduction in family income and a change of house. Paul learned early that if he wanted some special item—a telescope, for instance—he must work and save persistently for it himself. Milking cows at a penny apiece did not build a fortune overnight, but here was another seed forming Paul's character. God was teaching him to work hard to achieve his goals. In time he would transfer that principle to spiritual aims.

He became an achiever. Overcoming asthma and a weak right arm (the doctor who set a green-stick break did a sub-par job), Paul excelled as a long distance runner and held university and state records. Success on the oval gave him confidence. He learned the value of perseverance.

Perseverance also came into play when he asked Christ into his life. After signing the decision card taking God the Son to be his Savior, he felt no different. He might have faltered had not a school mate reminded him that his faith rested not on a feeling, but on God's promise. Soon afterward, he made an important decision: if he was going to be an active member of God's family, he "would do so in the full light of day." Immediately, he began telling others, including old Bill, the chemistry master, that he'd asked Jesus to run his life. Bill wasn't impressed. "Go for facts, White. That all sounds rather emotional . . . in anyone's thinking an empty tomb is a remarkably poor foundation for a religion. Now get on with your work."

Work Paul did—for the Lord. He continued to tell others of his faith and later became involved in the first Evangelical Union at Sydney University. He formed a definite picture of the work he hoped to do with his life. He wanted to become a missionary doctor to Africa. His resolve was tested when a laboratory job, promising badly needed income, was offered to him. Seeing it as a distraction from his purpose, he turned the offer down, although the medical career on which he was setting his sights was far from assured. Education was expensive. The only way he could attend university was by obtaining one of two hundred "exhibition" slots (a full-tuition scholarship). The rub was, Paul was not an ace student. His efforts seemed misdirected when he failed to matriculate at the appointed time. It took him an extra year of hard study before he won his "exhibition."

For four years he lived under an ax. Failure to pass even one of his exams would cut off his "exhibition" and end his career. Somehow he squeaked by. It meant stiff curtailment of his social calendar. He even had to ask Mary Bellingham, the girl he loved, to wait for three and a half years. He simply could not spare time for courtship, hope to pass his courses, and continue his involvement in campus youth outreach. Mary quietly agreed.

Three and a half years later, and not long before his final exams, Paul had the calm assurance he could ask Mary to become his wife. "Oh yes, yes," she replied. The pair basked in the glow of kisses, shared prayer, and dreams. A few days later Mary suffered the first of many traumatic bouts with manic-depression. Perhaps Paul's character never blazed brighter than at that moment. "If I make a promise while convinced of the rightness of a matter, I keep it. In spite of the apparent foolhardiness of the situation from a medical point of view, I really loved Mary and believed God had brought us together." He was in distress of spirit, and he yearned for Mary's recovery. Friends supported him as he struggled to prepare for his finals. He found concentration difficult on the oral exams. Yet, through those painful days, he could declare that God's support was almost tangible. Mary's ordeal—and his—lasted for three months.

Before marriage was possible, other work had to be done. The Lord provided Paul with experience that proved helpful in Africa. A stint as doctor during Queensland's rains prepared him for the sticky mud he would face in Africa's rainy season. A helpful mailman fed Paul a number of tips for makeshift devices to keep a vehicle running. And a ten-pound bonus provided Paul with the money for a honeymoon. A Sydney hospital job with a house became available. Paul and Mary married.

The Lord continued to open doors. A brother-in-law asked Paul to look after his general practice. This again provided needed income during the time when preparations for Africa began in earnest. Paul's student ministries had opened many doors for him, including invitations to speak on radio. He was able to bring the needs of Africa vividly before his listeners and was ahead of his time in breaking every need down into terms any listener could understand: six pounds and ten shillings will support a bed for a year, two shillings will deliver a baby, and so on. He bought or was given medicines, beds, power supplies, and surgical instruments. Thanks to the generosity of one Christian widow, Paul picked up one lot of instruments worth six hundred pounds for just five pounds.

When the Whites sailed for Tanganyika, their family included baby David. Rosemary would be born in Africa. Paul and Mary planned to serve out their lives in Africa. Mary wept when she saw their house; it was a disaster. Then putting a brave face to the situation, she began to make it into a home. Paul worked under primitive conditions and with a scarcity of supplies but was able to oversee the building of a new hospital at Mvumi, fifteen miles outside Dodoma (now the capital of Tanzania).

Again the Lord signaled change, this time on a trumpet. At times, Paul's asthma was so severe he had to be trundled to work in a wheelbarrow. Mary was desperately ill for eight months and her reason was restored only by what was then a new technique called Insulin Shock Therapy for Manic-Depressive Psychosis. Paul's friend Wellesly Hannah and a British doctor administered the treatment, following details they read in a medical article. Mary regained her mind for twelve hours then drifted back into psychosis. A second, desperate treatment restored her sanity. It was evident, however, that the Whites would have to return to Australia.

Just forty-two months after coming to Africa, the Whites found themselves aboard ship headed home to an uncertain future. As they sailed, Paul occupied his hours turning his notes of a medical safari into the book *Doctor of Tanganyika*. The book was well in hand when he disembarked with his family in Sydney. Almost immediately he was asked to take on a radio program, and the popular *Jungle Doctor* broadcasts began. In due course, a much needed income came his way when he was asked to work with a rheumatology specialist. And *Doctor of Tanganyika* was published despite wartime paper shortages.

Forty-two months of life in Africa had provided Paul with a rich fund of material. Without consciously intending to become a writer, he had made many notes. These inspired books, radio broadcasts, and comics. Wellesly also mailed interesting letters from Africa that provided Paul with grist for more writings. On later visits to Africa, Paul recorded background sounds that enlivened the radio programs, and he gathered film footage for TV shows. He also collected more story ideas—stories rich in parables of the kingdom of heaven. He wrote:

> The whites of many eyes stared at Daudi, the hospital dispenser, as he stood in the firelight, his finger raised.
>
> African night noises came on the night air.
>
> Daudi's deep voice started. . . .
>
> There was consternation in the jungle. All the animals met together one morning under the shade of a great buyu tree to see what could be done, for a great wall had suddenly appeared straight through the jungle.

Wellesly explained how the animals try to find a way through the wall because all of the best forest is on the other side. The rhinoceros charges the wall and bounces off. The elephant pushes against it with all his strength but cannot budge it. The hyena tries to find a secret path around but returns limping. The wall, it seems, goes on forever. The snake burrows deep into the earth but cannot find a hole through it. Nyani the monkey tries to climb it but loses his grip and plunges to earth.

> So the animals tried but there was no way through, under, over or around that Great Wall.
>
> Then they noticed the name of the wall for it was written in faint letters which could be seen only by those who understood.

The letters on the wall are S-I-N. And so began the *Jungle Doctor Fables*. Daudi had made a parable of the wall.

The thrust of Paul's life was to fight sin and its consequences.

"I'm a doctor. My job is to fight disease and its results in man's body and mind—the misery, pain, suffering, weakness, crippledom, confusion, death. What you mustn't forget or overlook is that sin is the disease of man's soul, a deadly thing." Disease and death are the unavoidable consequences of sin everywhere, but they bring aggravated misery when God's ways are forgotten. Witch doctors resisted not only the Christian gospel but also the medical relief that Christian doctors offered, and they often gave the worst possible treatment to medical problems. One witch doctor, for instance, treated eye disease by chewing up bark (her rotten teeth oozing pus), and spitting it into the suffering organ. In at least one instance, the eye became so infected that the eyeball swelled and burst.

Ignorance is another side effect of sin. Our understanding becomes darkened when we forget God. Paul White contended against this obstacle, too. His statistics showed that 780 of every thousand babies born to Tanganyikan mothers in his region died before they were a year old. This was largely the result of cramming gruel into the undeveloped stomachs of newborns. The hospital conducted a campaign to train African mothers to nurse their children with the motto "Breast feed is best feed and no porridge until the teeth come."

Paul conducted an unforgettable object lesson. He took ten children from the mission station and sat them beside ten children from the village. It was immediately apparent to everyone that the children who had been properly fed and bathed were much healthier than their village counterparts.

Paul and his African coworkers saw parables in the unlikeliest events. Once, the governor visited them unexpectedly. The clinic was a mess. Paul stalled the governor at the house while the staff rushed to tidy up. Much of the mess was quickly bundled into the dressing room—dirty dishes, soiled linens, mats, and beds.

"Bwana, whatever you do, do not enter the dressing room," entreated Dan.

The tour went without a hitch. The governor did not see the dressing room. Afterward, Dan came to Paul and said, "Bwana, truly today was a real parable. We were not fully prepared for the Governor's visit. I hope that it will teach me to be constantly ready to face my

Master, Jesus Christ, at any time, without having to bundle away a lot of things that I am ashamed of."

That particular incident found its way into *Doctor of Tanganyika.* It shows how Paul thought in pictures. Thirty similar word pictures found their way into *Get Moving,* a book of short, motivational parables on living the Christian life. Paul's word pictures made such an impression that people from around the world asked for them in their own languages, often doing the work of translation themselves. Today portions of Paul's writings appear in over one hundred languages in addition to their original English. In fact, apart from the Bible and John Bunyan, his writings are probably the most translated Christian literature in the world! This is because the stories have the same timeless quality as Aesop's fables. Always they drive home the point that people need Christ:

> Daudi nodded. "Truly sin is the great barrier which separates us from God. But there are those who know that this Great Wall has got a way through it. There is a door. Jesus, God's only Begotten Son, said, 'I am the door. By Me, if any man enter in, he shall be saved.' Why should we stay any longer on the wrong side of the wall?"

And as Paul noted, sin is no fun word to God. "The cost to God was infinite. The price to us is nothing. Closing our minds to this forgiveness is the supreme sin."

Paul's Christian outreach led him to become the Honorary General Secretary of Australia's InterVarsity Fellowship, the director of Christian publishing concerns, the author of a weekly column, and an editor. With David Britten, he co-authored Australian schoolboy stories with a Christian emphasis. Paul remained active with InterVarsity Fellowship, for a time as president, then as vice president until 1992. This work was accomplished despite asthma so severe it sometimes hospitalized him in a condition close to death. Fortunately, improved medications and the invention of inhalers eased his chronic ailment in later life.

After years of intermittent illness, Mary developed Alzheimer's disease. She had ceased to recognize Paul or her children before her death in 1970.

In 1971, Paul married Ruth Longe, who for several years had been his indispensable assistant and Mary's attendant. For most of their married life, he brought her breakfast in bed.

"He had an essential generosity," said Ruth. "He could have been a property millionaire but instead purchased land and buildings for various youth camps." The seeds of that generosity were planted in his youth. Even as a young boy he was taught to tithe. This practice and the giving of firstfruits remained with him all his life.

Paul was many-sided. "I believe wholeheartedly that there should be a time to play," he wrote. He loved to watch rugby football in the stands or on television. With Ruth, he enjoyed cricket. Catching his enthusiasm, she became hooked on bird-watching. Paul White Productions produced birdsong cassettes from Paul's bird-recording hobby. Paul also liked to cook and experiment with spices. His food did not always look the fanciest, but it was interesting!

Paul did not accomplish his lifework alone. If he grew up toward the measure of Christ, and to some extent fulfilled the Great Commission, it was because friends and contributors stood with him and were used by God in the turns of his life. He names many of his friends in *Alias Jungle Doctor* and was deeply attached to them. Paul himself embarked on what he called the *great safari* (life after death) in 1992.

Someday a trumpet will sound, signaling change for all the world. No one will be able to stop their ears to that blast. Then we will see what seeds each of us has sown and what crops each has reaped. Paul would ask, "Are you ready for that trumpet?"

30

Paul and Margaret Brand

(1914–) & (1919–)

Pioneers in the Treatment of Leprosy

*A man with leprosy came and knelt before him and
said, "Lord, if you are willing, you can make me
clean." Jesus reached out his hand and touched the
man. "I am willing," he said. (Matthew 8:2–3)*

Paul and Margaret Brand could serve as examples of
doctors as medical missionaries. Paul might equally well
represent the doctor as writer and apologist or skilled
surgeon. In this book, we focus on them as specialists.
In the medical field, their name is most often associated with work among leprosy patients.

Three men suffering with leprosy came for help one day to missionaries Jesse and Evelyn Brand. Fearful that son, Paul, and daughter, Connie, might contract the disease, which was thought to be highly contagious, the parents shooed the two children into the house. Paul, ever inquisitive, crept from his room and skulked behind rocks to watch as his parents fearfully approached the lepers to render what assistance they could. After the men had gone, the Brands burned a basket they had touched. They scrubbed themselves and changed their clothes. The children were forbidden to play where the three had squatted. Perhaps because of this incident, Paul developed a fear of leprosy while still young. It hardly presaged the work he was to do among those who suffered the horrible disease that seems to cause the body to rot away while it is living.

Apart from that incident, leprosy was not overly significant to the boy. Growing up in India, Paul led a largely unshackled childhood. He ran free, exploring the fascinating Indian environment and climbing trees at will. Trees were such a delight to him that his mother allowed him to study in one, lowering his completed homework to her in a basket. This was a wise decision, for book studies were not Paul's first love. It was not that his mind was slow but rather that he possessed a "hands-on" intelligence. There was much about which to be curious in his environment: scorpions, for instance, one of which stung him, or the snake that lived in a crack in the bathroom. Once, he succeeded in accidentally hanging himself while showing off. Connie's screams brought help in time to save his life.

In 1923, the Brands took Connie and Paul to England and left them there to study. Paul's restlessness continued to assert itself. He proved a poor student, glad merely to scrape by, yet feeling ashamed of his lack of attainment. Only the chance to escape into the countryside over holidays, to run free again as in India, sustained him.

Even though Paul planned to return to India as a missionary and had seen his father use medicine as a means of outreach, he refused to study medicine. His father's primitive doctoring and the nauseating sight of ulcers and pus appalled him. He wanted nothing to do with that kind of work. It was not that he preferred to preach and teach. Far from it. He understood himself well enough to know that he could not preach patiently for long years without visible results. No, he had to do something practical; he had to see tangible results. So he became a carpenter, building houses as had his grandfather, lay-preacher Henry Brand. The training was to prove useful in Paul's lifework.

If piety and fervor for souls characterized Paul's strict Baptist parents, it characterized him, too. He preached and taught Sunday school. In imitation of Christ's disciples, who set out two by two with virtually nothing, he took a ten-week, six hundred-mile evangelization trek along the Wales-England border, witnessing to people and living off whatever God provided him with. Few experiences could have better reinforced his faith.

Jesse Brand died suddenly when Paul was just fifteen years old. A telegram reached his two children in England at once. Letters written by their father and sent weeks before by surface mail continued to reach the Brand children in England, and Paul found it hard to believe that his father was dead. But when his mother returned from India, so aged by sorrow that the young man could scarcely recognize her, he had to accept the bitter truth. A hardness formed in him. He determined never to love anyone so totally, as his mother had loved his father, that death would leave him destroyed.

He applied to go as a missionary to India. To his surprise, the mission board turned him down. "Study medicine first," they advised him. Reluctantly, he signed up for a one-year course. To his astonishment, he found that he loved the work. Above all, the design of the human body deeply impressed him. After that, events led him into a full medical career. God, preparing him for a great work, placed him with some of the finest medical teachers in the nation. God also granted him extensive surgical experience when World War II broke out. Doctors were in such shortage because of war injuries that Paul found himself dealing with cases far in advance of his training. His workload would astonish our contemporaries.

Somehow he still found time for courtship. Falling in love with fellow student Margaret Berry, he married her during the war. Their first child, Christopher, was born during a bombing blitz.

Near the end of the war, Dr. Cochrane, a famed leprosy specialist and all-purpose doctor, urged Paul to join him in India. Indian independence was coming, and his medical college and hospital at Vellore needed more teachers in order to stay open. Paul doubted he could be released by the military authorities, who were still terribly short-handed. Dr. Cochrane replied, "Leave that to me." Cochrane was a man of deep Christian conviction who studied the Bible an hour each morning and two hours more, late each night. He was a man who let nothing stand in the way of God's will, banging on doors until he got what he needed. He wrangled Paul's release.

So Paul finally came back to his beloved India. In God's timing and with God's full preparation, he became a missionary doctor. Margaret, pregnant a second time, remained in England until after the baby was born.

Vellore is located about ninety miles from Madras. Its teaching hospital, founded by **Ida Scudder**, treated one hundred thousand patients a year. Paul was one of only three surgeons. Needless to say, his workload was heavy. Surgery usually began early in the morning and sometimes did not cease until late at night. In a nation that lacked sufficient trained doctors, there was always much more to be done than there was time to do it. Dr. Cochrane wore many hats and expected that Paul would, too. Among Cochrane's duties was the directorship of the Lady Willingden Leprosy Sanitarium. He took Paul on a tour of the facility. Would Paul not do something there? Paul was not interested.

He was not interested, that is, until he saw a pair of clawed hands and then several hands that had no fingers. Why did the hands of those who suffered leprosy twist up like that? he asked, and why did fingers fall off? No one knew. Cochrane himself—a leprosy expert who had pioneered the use of diaminodiphenylsulfone (DDS), the cheapest and purest of the sulfone drugs—had no idea. As a matter of fact, in spite of the millions of people in the world who suffered leprosy, no one understood certain puzzling features of the disease. Paul could not believe this astonishing fact until a study of the medical literature convinced him that Cochrane had spoken the truth. Amazed, Paul determined to solve at least some of the riddles.

He began studying leprosy in his "spare" time after teaching and operating for twelve hours a day. Others joined his effort. Soon he detected a pattern to the paralysis. It led him to ask if leprous flesh itself was rotten or if there was an external cause for the rotting? Paul sent sample after sample to specialists, and the verdicts came back again and again: nothing wrong with the flesh. This flew in the face of common assumptions. Everyone *knew* that leprous flesh was corrupt.

Gradually, Paul proved to a disbelieving medical establishment that victims of the disease lose their digits only because they cannot feel the damage they are doing to themselves. Leprosy deadens nerves. A patient would continue to walk on a sprained ankle, for instance, further tearing wounded tissues, because he is oblivious to pain that would make another person hobble to a seat and prop up the foot. Or a patient would leave a cut or a burn on a hand untreated and use the hand, so that the flesh was torn further and exposed to invasion by bacteria.

Advances in the treatment of leprosy had by then enabled doctors to slow the progress of, or even to cure, the disease. However, many of those who were cured retained deformities. A percentage of patients exhibited the clawed hands that had so intrigued Paul at the first. He believed that surgery could correct some leprous deformities. However, even at Vellore, where Paul's worth was well known, his insight was resisted. He was forbidden to allow leprosy patients into the wards. Finally, he obtained permission to admit one leprosy patient into a single-bed ward for an operation. By God's grace, the operation succeeded. Later, he discovered that that particular operation did not always succeed. But his initial success answered his critics and gave him courage to go on.

Before Paul attained this success, however, he had first to fit into the scene at Vellore and bring his family over to India. Margaret was still in England. Paul's in-laws, alarmed by India's postwar turmoil (which barely affected Vellore), pressured Margaret to remain in England. She hesitated to join Paul. This was partly his fault, for he had not answered her anxious questions about the situation, sending her cheery letters instead. She wrote him of her doubts. Disquieted, he telegrammed her to remain in England. Instead, her faith asserted itself and she came to India, ashamed for having doubted him. Soon, she became a co-laborer in the medical work, assisting as a volunteer in the pediatric department.

When the Brands' third child was born, Margaret took full-time leave. Within a fortnight, she received a note from the hospital director, "Margaret, we don't want to hurry you, but we are in desperate need of help in the eye department." She replied with an equally brief note, "I don't mind being hurried, but I know nothing about eyes. Please look for someone else." Medical training in war-torn Britain had been inadequate in some specialties. Back came a note: "You'll learn. Please start Monday." She had two whole days to bone up on ophthalmology!

About four hundred eye-patients, many with sight-threatening problems showed up that first Monday for treatment. "Talk about being thrown in at the deep end!" There was one doctor who knew something about ophthalmology and Margaret, who knew next to nothing, and had with her a two-week-old baby!

Margaret's situation eased some weeks later when Doctor Victor Rambo (1894–1987) returned from another assignment. Assuming she was no longer needed, Margaret went to say good-bye. Instead, Dr. Rambo convinced her to stay on. Helping as much as she could, without neglecting the family, Margaret became an enthusiastic eye specialist, marveling at God's design of that intricate organ. She worked beside Rambo at eye camps in local villages where upward of one hundred cataract surgeries a day might be performed.

At the end of one of these camps, as staff packed away instruments and equipment, Margaret noticed a group of people standing shyly to one side. She asked a camp worker who they were. Glancing at them the worker replied, "They are just lepers."

What did that mean? Did he mean, "We don't know what to do with them" or did he mean, "They don't matter that much"? Margaret took him with her to go look at them. Only one of them could see enough to lead the others. But as Margaret looked at their eyes, she realized she had seen nothing like them in her experience.

And so, as Paul had, Margaret found herself researching leprosy in medical literature. She found little to answer her questions. Like

Paul, she found that she must provide the answers herself. She became one of the first ophthalmologists to study large populations of lepers with eye problems (at the leprosy hospital near Vellore and at the National Leprosarium in Louisiana), eventually writing training manuals that are still in use around the world. She accomplished this despite maintaining a household and schooling the first four Brand children at home.

Meanwhile, Paul's work more and more included helping those who suffered from leprosy. Like other pioneers in the treatment of the disease, Paul found that he had to educate the medical community, which too often was not aware of the work that had already been done. The Norwegian Danielsen had carefully differentiated between leprosy and other diseases and described the two main types of the disease. His assistant, Hansen, had identified the bacillus that causes the disease. Others, such as Dr. Guy H. Faget in Louisiana, had found ways to administer sulfone drugs to kill the bacillus.

Paul developed statistics with care, knowing that the medical community must see the highest proof if long-held assumptions were to give way to truth. But mere records could not show the transformation that his work wrought in lives. Leprosy patients were taught to clean and inspect themselves daily, looking for wounds they could not feel. He showed them how to protect their deadened flesh from further injuries. Sometimes he managed surgically to correct the damage they had experienced. One technique was to transplant good muscles in place of those that had become paralyzed. Many of the patients became productive again. One man, with no more than finger stubs after treatment, was able to play the organ. Families were reunited after Paul assured them that leprosy is one of the least contagious of diseases. The Rockefeller Foundation heard of Paul's work and offered him a grant. He was uplifted.

Using a portion of the grant, he traveled to England and the United States, visiting nerve specialists. Perhaps their work would give him more clues to the baffling disease that destroys nerves. No one, it seemed, could help him discover the cause of the minute nodules he found in leprous nerves. No one, that is, until he spoke with Dr. Derek Denny-Browne. Browne had created such swellings in cats by diminishing blood to specific points in their bodies. This proved to be one more clue in explaining the effects of the disease.

To have leprosy is terrible. It is one of the few diseases in which the victim is named for his disease—"leper." It is a name that all who suffer from the disease plead to have abolished because of the stigma attached to it. Paul felt the awful weight of leprosy one night. He lost all feeling in a heel. Aware that leprosy attacks the extremities first, Paul immediately suspected that he had contracted the disease. He drove a pin deep into the affected part and could sense no pain. His suspicion was confirmed. Exhausted from his tour, mentally numbed by his terrible discovery, he threw himself on his bed. He was a leper!

The next morning, after a long, sleepless night, he decided to test the affected area again. Again he jabbed in a pin—and yelled with pain. Ever after he was to say, "Thank God for pain." In the previous night's mental fatigue, he had mistaken a foot fallen asleep for leprosy. Those terrible hours of fear taught him to empathize as never before with sufferers of the disease.

He returned to India better informed. There he designed new hospital buildings. His engineering experience proved invaluable. And he continued his work with leprosy patients. In this, too, his engineering experience proved of great value, for he was able to apply engineering ideas to the reconstruction of the body. His greatest contributions were to show how leprosy works and to find additional practical means to deal with the ravages of the disease. This is not to say that solutions came easily for Paul. It took him years of patient design and experimentation to build a shoe that would save a leper's unfeeling feet from damage.

His pioneer work did not go unnoticed. He was awarded the coveted Lasker Award, one of medicine's highest honors. Twice he was invited to give the prestigious John Hunter lecture. Queen Elizabeth II awarded him the CBE (Commander of the Order of the British Empire). Unaware that the Ambassador from Britain had arranged a big ceremony for handing over the insignia, he appeared in a rumpled, travel-soiled suit. The gaffe was graciously overlooked. His fame increased. Major medical centers offered him jobs (which he refused). Christ was not directing him toward these positions. His humility, however, could not prevent others from naming medical procedures after him.

Christians have a mixed record in the battle against leprosy. During the Middle Ages, the Church often anathematized lepers (going so far as to create a Leper's Mass, which cast out the sufferer). Individual Christians, however, such as St. Hedwig of Silesia, founded leprosariums. After 1100, a misinterpretation of Scripture effected a change in the treatment of lepers. People came to believe that Christ had suffered leprosy. The Order of St. Lazarus was founded to care for the pitiable outcasts. Queen Matilda washed their sores with her own hands. St. Francis of Assisi and Hugh of Lincoln were known for their sympathy toward the victims of leprosy.

Christians have been in the forefront of leprosy treatment ever since. Although neither Danielsen nor Hansen is known to have professed Christ, Damien the Priest woke the conscience of the world when he went to dwell among the leprous outcasts of Hawaii. It was the Daughters of Charity of St. Vincent de Paul who provided service to the lepers at Carville in Louisiana. Around the world, missionary doctors such as Ernest Muir, Frank Davey, and A. B. MacDonald shouldered the burden of helping the millions who suffer the disease. The load would have been unbearable apart from Christ. Yet, shoulder it they did, believing that "there can be no part-time workers for the Lord." Likewise, Paul Brand's work was an extension of his faith. He healed because Christ had healed.

Like Christ, he also preached. His favorite sermon was on hands— Christ's hands. He traced Christ's hands from uncontrolled infancy through skilled carpentry to the wrecked palms of crucifixion. Patients with leprosy, after hearing Paul's sermon on hands, held their damaged members with new dignity.

Paul developed other medical images and their analogy to the body of Christ in two powerful books he co-authored with Philip Yancy, *Fearfully and Wonderfully Made* and *In His Image*. He also wrote a book on suffering, *The Gift of Pain,* and one on spiritual food, *God's Forever Feast.*

A man's character is revealed not only in his work or his writings but also in his daily behavior. Those who labored beside Paul testify that he never became angry. Even in the most trying situations, he remained calm.

Leprosy is a cruel disease. It deforms and blinds its victims and often results in their segregation from society. Yet even the evil of leprosy can be used by the Lord. One of Margaret's most memorable patients was a high-caste Hindu and grade-A engineering student who contracted leprosy. Career, fiancée, family, and status were swept away at a blow. Angry and sick, he came to the leprosy hospital. When Margaret saw that his eyes were developing signs characteristic of loss of sight, she tried to prepare him for the worst. "Whatever happens, don't forget God loves you."

The man spat on the floor. "How can you say 'God loves you.' He has surely cursed me and taken from me everything I cherished."

Yet under the influence of Margaret and other dedicated caregivers, he softened and accepted the love of Christ. Dying of tuberculosis, he became a joyful witness for his Savior. In a letter that he wrote to Margaret, he said, "I am so glad I got leprosy. If I hadn't, I might never have heard of Jesus and what he has done for me. It was worth losing everything to have found him." Those who suffer leprosy around the world can testify that Christ's compassion was manifest in Paul and Margaret Brand and their fellow workers.

31

C. Everett Koop

(1916–)

Pediatrician and Surgeon General

*He will restore the hearts of the fathers to their
children. (Malachi 4:6* NASB*)*

As more and more types of surgery have been developed,
surgery has become increasingly specialized. C. Everett
Koop, with a deep love for children, became a pioneer in
pediatric surgery. As he wryly remarks in his memoirs,
pediatric surgery itself has since developed several
subspecialties. Koop represents the doctor as pediatrist.

W hy don't you go back where you came from? You're not needed
     here, you're not wanted here, and you put four good surgeons
out of work."

These were the words that greeted twenty-nine-year-old C. Everett
Koop on his first day at Philadelphia Children's Hospital. Not knowing it, he had stepped into a politically charged situation. General
surgeons, protective of their eroding turf, did not want to see another specialty carved off in pediatric surgery. So Koop found that,
rather than pour his full energy into developing new methods for
saving babies, he would have to expend effort to overcome opposition and outright hostility.

Koop set himself to win over the skeptics. Frustratingly, he was
frozen out of several urgent cases. Children died while doctors waged
a war of pride. In other instances, surgery had never before been
tried. "We just let those die—we can't fix them," he was told. Despite the risk of sailing into uncharted waters, Koop attempted to
save little lives, using common sense and courage. In this way, he
became one of the great innovators in the field of pediatrics. Many
of his methods became commonplace. "The surgical care of newborns now seems so routine that it is hard to believe it did not exist
in 1946 when I started work at Children's Hospital of Philadelphia,"
he recalled.

After finding a safe way to administer anesthesia to newborn babies through the trachea, Koop and his team turned to surgical methods for correcting congenital birth defects. These problems included
water on the brain, inguinal hernia, and defects in which the esopha-
gus was incomplete or did not join the stomach. Hernia surgery on
children became so routine that he reduced its time to six minutes
and perfected it so thoroughly that the child could engage in normal
play the same day. At the other end of the pediatrician's spectrum,
he founded the nation's first neonatal intensive care unit.

Asked if he thought his Christian belief helped him in surgery,
Doctor C. Everett Koop replied, "Without any question. The things
that I do deal with life and death. I often encounter the agony of
parents separated from their children by death or facing difficult
problems with malformation. . . . If I didn't believe that I had a God

who was solid and dependable, a God who makes no mistakes, I couldn't continue what I'm doing. I need that certainty to assure me that what I'm doing is the right thing, and I need it in my day-to-day existence with all the problems that I personally face. I would have a great deal of trouble with them if I didn't have complete faith in Jesus Christ."

C. Everett Koop learned faith in Christ when he was about thirty— at almost the same time he became surgeon in chief of the Children's Hospital of Philadelphia. During his struggles for acceptance from his medical peers, he also was groping for spiritual meaning. The medical ice broke one day when he made a judicious call on a baby. Other doctors had wanted to drain some pus from beneath the child's lung with a needle. Koop, or "Chick," as he was called, showed that the X-rays had been misread. The pus was in a cyst *within* the lung. Using a needle could have caused a deadly hemorrhage. After that, he sensed a new respect from his colleagues. The spiritual ice thawed over a period of several months under the teaching of Presbyterian minister Donald Grey Barnhouse. This intelligent and service-oriented Christian convinced Koop that real faith was possible. Koop had been a churchgoer all of his life but had never truly assimilated the message of redemption.

> Over those several months, sitting in the balcony at the Tenth Presbyterian Church, the preaching from the pulpit made it all clear: that the essence of Christianity was not what we did, but what Christ had done for us. I understood the meaning of Christ's sacrifice, I understood the meaning of divine forgiveness. I realized that either my sins were on my shoulders, or they were on the shoulders of Jesus Christ. I saw how the atonement of Jesus Christ was necessary to reconcile us to God.

It was not that Koop hadn't tried to live a decent life. Born in Brooklyn in 1916, he knew from an early age what he wanted to be—a doctor. The doctors he had known seemed the most wonderful people in the world to him. One of them, his Uncle Henry, cured pernicious anemia with ground liver sausage decades before a Nobel prize was given to another man for the same discovery. Because Koop was clever with his hands, he wanted to be not just a doctor but a surgeon. Such was his dedication to his goal that as a boy he practiced for hours cutting pictures out of magazines with scissors and tying one-handed knots using either his left hand or his right hand to train himself to be ambidextrous.

While still a young teen, he worked without pay at the Mather Memorial Hospital. He was not even fourteen when he talked a surgeon into letting him observe his first operation. Because he was a large boy, he was soon able to con his way into the surgical theater of Columbia's Presbyterian Hospital as a medical student and see all of the surgery he wanted. With his mother acting as anesthesiologist, he began practicing operations at home on rats and rabbits. At sixteen, he took his first summer job in a hospital.

His longing to become a surgeon was great. In an autobiographical essay written at sixteen, he said he hoped to attend Dartmouth College. But he committed his plans to "One whose infinite wisdom guides our lives for the best." That One allowed him, through a doctor who believed in him, to perform a leg amputation under supervision when he was just nineteen.

Koop did make it to Dartmouth. As he tells it, he prepared for college by learning every fight song of the college. That was the kind of enthusiasm he brought to every undertaking in his life. He went out for football. Knocked cold on the field, he awoke seeing double. The double vision remained all of his life. Rather than risk his surgical career with another damaging hit, he made one of the most difficult decisions of his life and quit football.

One of his college jobs was to feed *Ablystoma notatum,* tiny vertebrates on which a professor was experimenting with lens transplants. Again, Koop recognized God's oversight of his life. Tedious and painstaking, the job helped prepare him for pediatric surgery.

God's watchfulness was again at work when Koop sought entrance into Columbia's College of Physicians and Surgeons. They told him, "We don't think you have the stuff we are looking for." Disappointed, he accepted Cornell University Medical College's subsequent offer. The change of plans turned out for the best. He found the atmosphere at Cornell more congenial, especially when he broke a leg skiing and had to be helped by classmates for several months. He realized that God had directed him where He wanted him, for he would probably have had to drop out of arrogant, competitive Columbia.

Koop was a risk taker. Sometimes this endangered his chances of a medical career. Not only did he break his leg skiing, but he also broke his neck and once suffered frostbite to his hands. By marrying Betty Flanagan before he was through medical school, he seriously jeopardized his chances of an internship—the schools were prejudiced against married students. While a fourth-year student, he delivered a baby in a tenement and then took the risk of repairing the mother on the spot. She was so badly torn from previous childbirths that she needed immediate surgery. The resident who was supposed to back him up had lazily sent him off alone with the medical bag. If infection had set in and the woman had died, Koop would have been in serious trouble. He took the risk because he knew that he could never have persuaded her to come to the hospital.

In time, Koop became noted for his pioneer work in pediatrics. The mortality rate for many of the surgeries he pioneered was 95 percent when he took over. When he retired, the survival rate from his improved procedures was 95 percent. He also gained fame separating Siamese twins.

During this time, he won respect in the evangelical community. He had treated Frankie Schaeffer, son of evangelist and Christian apologist Francis Schaeffer, for post-polio foot. Years later, he and Francis Schaeffer happened to meet as speakers on the same Canadian campus. Shortly afterward, they teamed up to produce the video series *Whatever Happened to the Human Race?* which championed life against the forces of abortion and euthanasia.

Koop's worldwide recognition as a champion for the unborn and the vulnerable led to his nomination as surgeon general early in Ronald Reagan's presidency. From first to last, Koop stood against the cheapening of human life. In addition to making the video series *Whatever Happened to the Human Race?* Koop wrote his antiabortion tract *The Right to Live, the Right to Die* and published an article titled "The Slide to Auschwitz," which Ronald Reagan reprinted as a chapter in his little book *Abortion and the Conscience of a Nation.* Koop saw abortion as leading down a slippery path to infanticide and euthanasia. These views made him especially desirable to the Reagan administration, but they also made him anathema to pro-choice constituencies.

Every fight of Koop's past paled beside the battle for confirmation as surgeon general. Planned Parenthood, the National Abortion Rights League, the National Organization of Women, and other related groups fought his nomination with a vicious smear campaign. Newspapers called him "Doctor Kook" without so much as an attempt to contact him for his side of the story. At times, he was tempted to withdraw his nomination, but "I felt the Lord's assurance when I needed it the most." His confirmation was eleven months in coming.

One of Koop's first tasks was to revitalize the demoralized Commissioned Corps, which had suffered funding cuts and the closure of numerous facilities. As surgeon general, Koop stepped back from the abortion battle. To emphasize this divisive issue would be counter-productive to other efforts that he undertook, including, for instance, his battle against smoking, which antagonized Reagan's tobacco-growing constituents. Perhaps Koop's most controversial decision was his attempt to educate Americans on the topic of acquired immuned deficiency syndrome (AIDS). This effort outraged the religious right because, while advocating abstinence outside of marriage, it also urged those who practiced promiscuity to at least use condoms to reduce the chances of spreading the deadly virus. His battle for the rights of the handicapped also offended a growing number of people who valued "quality" of life above life itself. He predicted the rise of euthanasia in the 1990s.

Koop battled other not-so-obvious health concerns. He convened a conference against family violence. He wrote and spoke against pornography, especially child porn, which leaves many children socially crippled—if their lives are not altogether snuffed out by the pornographers.

Children were always important to Koop. For the sake of other people's children, he often had to give up time with his own. To compensate, he made it a point always to be at home for evening dinner if humanly possible. So that his children could have a sense of sharing in his work, he brought home pictures and slides showing what he was doing. Every summer, he took his family on a four- or five-week vacation in New Hampshire. The accidental death of their son David was a terrible blow to Betty and Koop. Koop's concern for children, both the born and the unborn, made him an admirable and humane man opposed to many trends of our day.

32

Paul Carlson

(1928–1964)

Monganga Paulo, Congo Doctor

Greater love has no one than this, that he lay down his life for his friends. (John 15:13)

Paul Carlson was a missionary doctor. When the Simba rebels drew near, he could have run. Instead, he chose to stay as long as he could with his African patients. One hundred thousand people looked to him as their only doctor. His concern for others proved fatal to him. The rebels captured, beat, and ultimately killed him. Many doctors have given their lives for their patients. Paul Carlson was killed because he had chosen to follow Christ. He represents the doctor as martyr.

My husband came here because he loved you. He saw the great medical need and wanted to serve, both medically and spiritually. Why his time was so short among you, we do not know. But God knows."

Soldiers ringed the church as Lois Carlson spoke these words at the funeral of *Monganga Paulo,* "My Doctor Paul." Rebellion had brought turmoil to the former Belgian Congo (Zaire). Paul Carlson's coffin was mute testimony to the heartache the rebellion was leaving in its wake.

Lois might not have known why Paul's time was so short, but already there were hints of God's greater plan. His martyrdom was a testimony even at his funeral. Pastor Zacharie Alengie reminded the listeners of the noble work Paul had done among them, his love, his smile, and his willingness to go the extra mile even when he was bone tired.

"Why did this doctor choose a place like this?" asked Alengie. He answered his own question. "It came from love and joy." And then he asked the most pertinent question of all: "On the day of resurrection, will you see the doctor?" Yes. Because of his self-sacrificing character, Paul's Christian faith was reaching out to more souls in death than it had in life.

And not just in the Congo. A concatenation of providential circumstances brought him to world attention in a way that increased the impact of his death.

Paul was born at midnight on March 28, 1928, and his parents dedicated him to the Lord's use. At twelve years of age he gave his heart to Christ and was later an enthusiastic participant in the youth group of the First Covenant Church of Los Angeles. An evangelistic mind-set formed in him. He suggested that members of the youth group reach out to servicemen in the Los Angeles area, and they did. Around that same time, Paul dedicated his life to missionary work after hearing a missionary speaker. A youth counselor at a church camp that Paul attended was studying medicine; this may have sparked Paul's interest in the field. At any rate, he was soon making plans to become a doctor. After a two-year stint in the navy, Paul headed to college. He met Lois while he worked as an orderly. She had recently received her nurse's cap.

Lois was attracted to him. They began sharing long talks, Campus Crusade activities, and prayer. Lois knew that if she married Paul, she also would be marrying adventure and probably medical missionary work. She was not sure this was what she wanted. But she became his wife because she knew that he was the sort of man with whom she wished to spend her life.

The two shared the typical struggles of newlyweds when one partner is in medical school. They had to find apartments, stretch their small budget to cover endless expenses, and catch moments together on the fly. There were moves as Paul's studies and internship bounced them coast to coast. There were triumphs and discouragements. Children arrived. At one point, Paul questioned the grounds of his faith. The Lord brought him through that test more convinced than ever of the truth of Christianity. Paul was greatly used when the Covenant church lost its pastor. Since it would be several months before a new man could come, and the church was beginning to drift, Paul felt called to stir up the congregation to pray and to embark on "One Hundred Days of Preparation" for the coming of the new leader. By keeping close contact with their coming pastor, the leaders had the church prepared to hit the ground running the moment the new man arrived.

At the very moment when it appeared that Paul and Lois could settle down and reap the rewards of his education—they had finally bought their very own California home—Paul responded to a plea by the Protestant Relief Agency for short-term doctors in the Congo. Seven hundred Belgian doctors had fled the Congo when it was granted independence, leaving a crisis in medical care. Paul and a few other volunteers strove valiantly to plug the gap left in health care by those desertions. When his six months were up, he returned to the States elated. He had loved the work despite the primitive conditions and lack of equipment. His vision of Christian medical work was restored. There could be little doubt that he would say "yes" when the Congolese church itself requested him as their permanent medical staffer.

So the Carlsons found themselves in 1963 adjusting to life in the Congo. Whereas in America there was one doctor for every seven hundred people, in the Congo there was only one doctor for every one hundred thousand people. Paul found himself working long hours under a constant barrage of petty inconveniences, equipment breakdowns, and supply shortages. His faith and determination to succeed merely increased as he performed emergency surgery by flashlight in desperate weariness.

Paul was not immune to these troubles. Philip Littleford, a student who worked with him, would later write, "Since Paul's death there has been a tendency to look at him as a little more than human. He was in fact very human. He would get angry, discouraged, and frustrated. But that was the marvel of it—for Christ's love was evident in him despite these frailties. His first love was Christ, and to say that this was evident is the greatest tribute one can make."

Paul's work was performed against a background of political unrest. The Carlsons were not greatly disturbed. Wasolo, their station, was in the far north of the Congo, out of the mainstream of events. Nonetheless, they could not avoid some sense of concern. In 1963, the United Nations had intervened in the Congo situation. When its troops pulled out, rebel Simbas, sponsored by Red China, seized increasing chunks of territory. The Congolese National Army was not able to put up effective resistance. The government of Moshe Tsombe tottered. The political and military situation remained tense throughout 1964.

Paul spoke at the Wasolo Regional Church Conference. "We do not know what will happen in 1964—and in 1965—until we meet together again. We do not know if we will have to suffer and die during this year because we are Christians. But it does not matter! Our job is to follow Jesus."

Just how he followed Christ was revealed to the world through another providential event. Doctor Warren Berggren, also working in the Congo, had promised to sponsor a senior medical student from Johns Hopkins University under a fellowship granted by Smith, Kline and French laboratories. Now Berggren became seriously ill; he would have to leave the Congo. Paul agreed to sponsor the student, Philip Littleford, in Berggren's stead. So, as the rebellion came to crisis, photographers and news writers produced a story on Phil Littleford and his sponsor, Paul Carlson.

On August 6, 1964, Stanleyville (Kisangani) fell to the rebels. Embassies warned foreigners to pull out. Paul took Lois and the children to safety across the Ubangi River into nearby Central African Republic. He returned to his duties at Wasolo. Urgent cases remained, people who would die without his attention. His decision was dangerous but not an act of bravado. Rebels had not molested doctors so far. And Wasolo was only an hour from the safety of the Central African Republic.

On September 18, the rebels, hard-pressed by developments, shot to death two of Paul's Congolese coworkers and seized Paul as a hostage. He was but one of several hundred white people held throughout the Congo. Nonetheless, because of his recent press exposure, he became the face of all the hostages.

The Simbas accused Paul of being an American mercenary. They said that he was calling in American planes when he used his radio transmitter. His captors singled him out for beatings. In these desperate moments, Paul proved that his faith was not mere words. He pleaded for the lives of three Catholic missionaries, all of them injured through mistreatment by the Simbas. He won their freedom. Beaten, he tended to the ailments of the very men who had tormented him. He returned to his fellow hostages in pain, yet it was he who comforted them. He had the New Testament in his possession. Now he pored over its passages whenever he could and derived strength from his reading. The captive missionaries stayed near each other for prayer and Bible study.

Paul was brought to Stanleyville. He was sentenced to death as an American spy, reprieved, threatened with death, reprieved again, depending on whether events were going badly or well for the rebels. The United States threatened intervention. The Simbas promised death to their 250 Stanleyville hostages if any rescue was attempted.

On the morning of November 24, airplanes roared over Stanleyville. American C-130 transports dropped Belgian crack paratroops into the city. The prisoners were marched out of their barracks, an old hotel. "*Ciyuga! Ciyuga!*" called radio Stanleyville. "Kill them all!" The panicked rebels began to fire. Many of the hostages bolted to cover. Several of the Americans ran for a wall.

They vaulted to shelter behind it. Paul also leaped for the wall—but too late. A young Simba warrior withered him with machine gun fire. Photographs showed Paul Carlson lying dead on the pavement, his vacant eyes staring forever beyond the camera.

Paul was one of sixty foreigners who died. Hundreds of Congolese also died, some for their faith, some merely because they had a little more substance than others, were better educated, or favored Western policies over communism. They did not appear on the cover of *Time.* It was Paul, with his faith, his love for the Congolese, and his concern for Congolese health who was there.

His life remained a testimony to Christ even in his death.

Thumbnail Sketches

While researching these chapters, I found information on a number of other health workers who were Christians. Had I attempted to write about all of them, this book would have quickly grown too large to print. All the same, I want to share the Christian conviction of these other notable medical workers; therefore, I have prepared this dictionary of names. No doubt many more names could have been included, and I apologize to the memory of all the fine Christian men and women who made outstanding contributions to medicine but are overlooked here.

GEORGIAS AGRICOLA (1494–1555)

Agricola trained as a medical doctor but is better known as the Father of Metallurgy. He was especially interested in the treatment of the diseases of miners. A Roman Catholic, he was highly respected by Protestants and Catholics alike.

SIR THOMAS BARLOW (1845–1945)

Barlow differentiated childhood scurvy from rickets. Because of his work, scurvy is sometimes called "Barlow's Disease." Reared Wesleyan, he remained a Methodist until middle age, when a close friendship with a Church of England vicar led him to change churches. He was a man of piety and kindness. Hardworking and patient, he possessed a great sympathy for his patients, especially children. His colleagues held him in high esteem. He served as president of the Royal College of Physicians and in other notable roles.

THOMAS BARNARDO (1845–1905)

Thomas Barnardo completed three years of a four-year medical course. Becoming involved in relief of poor boys, he left school to concentrate on that work. He developed many homes and ministries for the poor. His assumption of the title "doctor" raised the ire of critics because he had not completed his training, although the training he completed made him better educated than any doctor of antiquity.

BENJAMIN BARTON (1766–1815)

Benjamin Barton is credited with writing the first botany textbook in America. He was a creationist and was especially interested in the relations and dispersion of the human race, which he believed took place after the Noahic flood. After taking his M.D. degree (studying at Edinburgh, London, and Göttingen), Barton taught at the University of Philadelphia. He prepared a collection of material on American *materia medica.*

SAINT BASIL (ca. 329–379)

St. Basil founded many hospital-like institutions. They did not provide medicine so much as places for the sick to lie. Well educated, Basil contended against Arianism (a cult that denied Christ's full divinity). He promoted monasticism and learning.

THOMAS BATEMAN (1778–1821)

Thomas Bateman is best known as one of the first dermatologists. After a life of skepticism, Bateman was prompted to inquire into the tenets of Christianity by a serious illness. He acknowledged his sin, repented heartily, embraced Christ's redemptive work, and left a written record of his changed views.

ELIZABETH BLACKWELL (1821–1910)

Elizabeth Blackwell was the first American woman to graduate from a medical school. She was confirmed within the Christian communion but drifted toward the "rational" Christianity of Swedenborg.

TIMOTHIE BRIGHT (1551–1615)

During the St. Bartholomew's Day Massacre, in which Catholics killed Huguenots and other Protestants, Timothie Bright was in Paris. He had to flee to the residence of the British Ambassador for safety. Thereafter, he was a vocal opponent of Roman Catholicism. Bright was a physician but is better remembered as the inventor of the first modern shorthand and the editor of the first abridged version of Foxe's *Actes and Monuments,* better known as the *Book of Martyrs.* Additionally, Bright wrote a treatise on melancholy. Burton's *Anatomy of Melancholy* followed Bright's plan chapter by chapter.

THOMAS BROWNE (1605–1682)

The author of *Religio Medici* was a physician. *Religio Medici* opens with an avowal of Christianity and continues in the same vein. Thomas Browne favored the forms of the Church of England.

WILLIAM BROWNRIGG (1711–1800)

William Brownrigg is little known, despite having done research of great merit into the oxides of carbon. His lack of renown is because he could never be persuaded to publish his findings, although he frequently advised coal miners regarding "fire-damp" in their mines. A benevolent, learned, and humane physician, Brownrigg was also a firm believer in Christianity.

CASSIODORUS (490–ca. 585)

Cassiodorus, a highly placed court official and the close friend of the theologian-philosopher Boethius, founded two monasteries. He required his monks to copy texts of ancient books, among which were medical works. Despite the skeptical attitude of the church toward Hippocrates's books, Cassiodorus urged their use. He also advocated the use of medical illustrations.

EDITH CAVELL (1865–1915)

As a prominent nurse, Edith Cavell ran an innovative nursing establishment in Belgium, which she converted to a hospital at the onset of World War I. She was accused of assisting allies to escape back to their lines and of helping Belgian youths avoid military draft by the Germans and was convicted and shot. Before her death she remarked, "I have seen death so often that it is not strange or fearful to me. Standing as I do in view of God and eternity, I realize patriotism is not enough. I must have no hatred or bitterness toward anyone."

WALTER CHARLETON (1619–1707)

President of the Royal College of Physicians, Walter Charleton also was a defender of biblical miracles, creationism, and the Flood.

SIR ROBERT CHRISTISON (1797–1882)

Sir Robert Christison established the scientific basis of medical jurisprudence while he was a professor at Edinburgh. He gave precise, lucid medical testimony in many important cases in Scotland and England, and learned to distinguish carefully between wounds inflicted before death and those inflicted after death. His book on poisons was of immediate value. He also did important work on diseases of the kidneys, measurement of the ages of trees, and more. Despite his heavy research, he found time to conduct an extensive private practice and to serve as an elder in the Scottish church.

WILLIAM FAIRLUE CLARKE (1833–1884)

Diseases of the tongue were of special interest to William Fairlue Clarke; he published a well-received volume on the subject. His *Manual of the Practice of Surgery* was so useful that it went through three editions. Convinced at an early age of the importance of Christianity, Clarke held firm religious convictions all of his life. The Medical Missionary Association carried on, under his name, a work that he had begun, bringing together medical students annually.

WILLIAM SANDS COX (1802–1875)

William Sands Cox founded Queen's College, Birmingham, originally known as the Birmingham School of Medicine. Later, through his efforts and those of Reverend Warneford, it was extended to encompass theology and the liberal arts. Cox also founded the organization that became the British Medical Association. A skilled surgeon, Cox was also a strong churchman. At his death, he gave a good deal of money not only to medical scholarships but also to establish and support dispensaries in Birmingham's suburbs.

M. R. DE HAAN (1891–1964)

M. R. DeHaan gave up medical practice to become a pastor and was the founder of *Radio Bible Class*.

SAINT VINCENT DE PAUL (1581–1660)

Vincent de Paul was a Catholic reformer and the cofounder of the nursing group, the Sisters of Charity. The sisters operated the hospitals and pharmacies of prerevolutionary France.

TOM DOOLEY (1927–1961)

Remembered as the author of a series of books that he published about his work in Southeast Asia (*Deliver Us from Evil, Before I Sleep,* and so on), Tom Dooley was staunchly Roman Catholic. He was interested in providing medical care to underdeveloped countries and implemented public health measures in North Vietnam in 1954. From his book royalties, he established a hospital in Laos. MEDICO, an organization he founded, provides medical facilities in needy countries.

DANIEL DRAKE (1785–1852)

Founder of the Medical School of Ohio, Daniel Drake was a tireless proponent of medical education. He edited the *Western Medical and Physical Journal.* Although he claimed Christ, he had a highly contentious nature.

HENRI DUNANT (1828–1910)

Swiss banker and evangelical Christian Henri Dunant was inspired to found the Red Cross. Dunant witnessed a terrible battle in Italy and assisted with the care of the wounded for weeks afterward. He realized that if even minimal medical services had been ready, much needless suffering could have been prevented. Filled with a sense that God wanted him to do something about the problem, he wrote a book, *Memory of Solferino*, which electrified public attention. "I was aware of an intuition, vague and yet profound, that my work was an instrument of His will," he said. He suggested the first international alliance of the world's Young Men's Christian Associations (YMCAs) and wrote their charter. At that time, the YMCA was still an evangelical organization.

THEODOR FLIEDNER (1800–1864)

Theodor Fliedner was a German Lutheran minister. He did much philanthropic work and pioneered the training of nurses. Elizabeth Fry (1780–1845) was acquainted with him because of their shared interest in prison reform.

SIR JOHN FLOYER (1649–1734)

John Floyer's name is linked with hydrotherapy and spa treatments. He also wrote about the pulse, which he took by the minute, and about asthma. Samuel Johnson, the famed man of literature, respected Floyer so highly that he urged an editor to prepare an account for the public of Floyer's "learning and piety."

STEPHEN HALES (1677–1761)

Although not a physician, the Reverend Stephen Hales did notable work on the study of blood pressure, devising many clever experiments, such as attaching a tall glass tube to the carotid artery of a horse to see how high the pulses of its heart would drive the blood. Hales was a genuinely Christian man who poured himself out for the good of others. It is not possible here to list all of his charitable, scientific, and religious activities. Suffice it to say that he was an active proponent of practical prison and hospital reform, pressing to have fresh air brought to inmates and patients through ventilators. Alexander Pope, the quarrelsome poet, described his neighbor Hales as always serene and cheerful.

WILLIAM HARVEY (1578–1657)

Famed as the first anatomist to demonstrate the circulation of the blood through the arteries and veins, William Harvey spoke so little of his faith that John Maynard Keynes found small evidence of it to include in his biography. However, the poet Abraham Cowley wrote an elegy on the great man, his friend, in which he says:

> With as much zeal, devotion, piety
> He always lived, as other saints do die
> Still with his soul severe accounts he kept
> Weeping all debts out, ere he slept.

JOHANNES BAPTISTA VAN HELMONT (1579–1644)

The founder of pneumatic chemistry and chemical physiology, Johannes Baptista van Helmont was committed to the Christian revelation. He undertook his work with gases (he gave us the word *gas,* from the Dutch *gaas,* "chaos") in an effort to discover the soul. He thought that because

God had breathed life into Adam, the seat of the soul might be found by a close study of air.

ROBERT HEMPHILL (flourished 1660)

Robert Hemphill was a clergyman and physician. He migrated to America to obtain religious freedom. He had hidden his Bible in a hollow log on the bank of Loch Neigh and later made a round trip of six thousand miles to recover it and return with it to the New World. That Bible is a prized possession of his descendants.

HILDEGARD OF BINGEN (died 1179)

Hildegard of Bingen wrote an encyclopedia of natural sciences and clinical medicine. Along with large doses of mysticism and exorcism, it included shrewd observations and herbal formulas. She is credited with a number of highly original ideas, especially in the area of psychology. Some people have called her the most important medical writer of the Middle Ages. A mystic and a prophetess, she was highly influential in her era.

JAMES HINTON (1822–1875)

James Hinton, after renouncing Christianity, returned to it and became, in his own words, "a Christian of sorts." He concerned himself with unfortunates, such as slaves. Finding that life in business did not suit him, he turned to medicine. He was notable in the practice of surgery on the ear.

WILLIAM WILLIAMS KEEN JR. (1837–1932)

William Keen's *System of Surgery,* in eight volumes, was the bible of American surgeons for decades. He had the best of all classrooms: the hospitals of America's Civil War. An innovator, he undertook brilliant new surgeries on the brain. Although he accepted theistic evolution and even wrote in its defense, he was ardently committed to the Christian faith, of which he often spoke. "He is the best physician who takes account of the life hereafter as well as the life that now is, and who not only heals the body but helps the soul. . . ."

JOHN KIDD (1775–1851)

Chosen to write one of the Bridgewater Treatises, John Kidd titled his essay *The Adaptation of Nature to the Physical Condition of Man.* He was an M.D., but he is best remembered for his work with coal as a source of chemicals.

ATHANASIUS KIRCHER (1602–1680)

Athanasius Kircher was a Jesuit and a polymath—a man who turned his mind to every field of thought of his day and made contributions in each. One of his fields of interest was medicine.

JACQUES-DESIRE LAVAL (1803–1864)

Jacques-Desire Laval found that doctoring did not satsify his soul. Consequently, he entered seminary. Eventually he became a priest to the island of Mauritius. His holiness led to the conversion of thousands. Today he is revered by Protestant, Catholic, Muslim, and other islanders alike. "Religion divides, holiness unites," observed a priest who came after him. The date of his death, the ninth of September, is a Mauritian national holiday.

CAROLUS LINNAEUS (1707–1778)

Famed for his system of classification of plants, Linnaeus was trained as a medical doctor and held a professorship of medicine at Uppsala, Sweden. His works abound in exclamations of praise to God the Creator.

D. MARTYN LLOYD-JONES (1899–1981)

The Welsh doctor-turned-minister Martyn Lloyd-Jones is famed for his scriptural commentaries and the education of preachers. He was a brilliant and God-fearing man, one of the great names in twentieth-century faith.

JOHN LOCKE (1632–1704)

Although remembered today as a philosopher, John Locke practiced medicine. In those loose days, many educated and uneducated men did so, even without taking medical degrees. Locke, a Christian, argued vehemently against Deism (which accepts the existence of a distant God but ignores Christ). Although he denied the inspiration of selected passages in Paul's letters, he wrote a treatise on the *Reasonableness of Christianity*, which is not as famous as his *Two Treatises on Government* or his *Essay on Human Understanding*. As he lay dying, he asked that a clergyman give him the sacrament at home, and he requested that Lady Masham read psalms to him. She did until he quietly drew his last breath.

ROSALIE SLAUGHTER MORTON (1876–?)

Reared as a Quaker, Rosalie Slaughter Morton gives in her autobiography, *A Woman Surgeon: The Life and Work of Rosalie Slaughter Morton*, the vivid details of her courageous entry into the medical profession against considerable opposition. She was the first woman to undertake surgery in Washington. She was active as a surgeon on the front during World War I. At her Christian marriage ceremony, she refused to promise "to obey" her husband, believing that each individual's conscience must rather be obedient to God.

RICHARD LOWER (1631–1691)

Richard Lower was the pupil of the celebrated Thomas Willis and assisted him in his anatomical studies. He is perhaps most famous for his experiments with blood transfusion. Not enough was then known about the differences in blood types to make transfusion reliable. Lower was a physician with strong Protestant beliefs, and his fortunes rose and ebbed according to who held power. In the end, he was deprived of his position, and his medical practice declined because of court disapproval. His will left money to assist French and Irish Protestants who had become refugees from Catholic lands for their faith. He also left money for St. Bartholomew's Hospital.

EPHRAIM MCDOWELL (1771–1830)

Ephraim McDowell, a doctor on the Kentucky frontier, performed the world's first known successful ovariotomy. Reared as a strict Presbyterian, he transferred his allegiance to the milder Episcopal denomination, founding its Dansville church. He preferred to operate on Sundays so that parishioners could back him up with prayer. Almost all of his abdominal surgeries were successful, but many of his contemporaries bitterly opposed them. In the end, he gave up medicine for the life of a Southern planter.

S. WEIR MITCHELL (1829–1914)

S. Weir Mitchell spoke little of his faith, but he had been reared as a Quaker and sometimes wondered aloud how a person could live without Christ. An American doctor, he was in the forefront of studies of psychiatric illnesses and problems. He also produced numerous novels, poems, and plays. Some of the novels became best-sellers. Although rather wooden, these works retain sufficient merit that Mitchell is included in Twayne's American Authors series. His works sometimes express Christian themes. Freud drew on Mitchell's studies in creating his own better-known theories.

SAMUEL A. MUDD (1833–1883)

Samuel A. Mudd was accused of complicity in the assassination of Abraham Lincoln because he treated the fleeing actor-assassin, John Wilkes Booth. For many years, Mudd served as physician to his fellow prisoners. He was sustained through his unjust imprisonment by his Christian faith.

FLORENCE NIGHTINGALE (1820–1910)

Florence Nightingale is famous as the "Lady with the Lamp." Her reforms of military nursing had a tremendous impact on the world. She wrote hundreds of thousands of words of unorthodox Christian theology, but there is no doubt that she was inspired by Christ and Theodore Fliedner to undertake her noble work.

JOHN BELL PETTIGREW (1834–1908)

An outstanding anatomist, John Bell Pettigrew amassed a huge amount of evidence for human and animal design by a creator. He published these findings in a treatise titled *Design in Nature*.

WILLIAM PETTY (1623–1687)

William Petty is remembered for his association with Robert Boyle, Christopher Wren, and other early members of the Royal Society. A physician, he employed his great and original intelligence toward founding the sciences of statistics and economics and was long credited with statistical work actually done by John Graunt. Petty also wrote on design in nature.

PHILIPPE PINEL (1745–1826)

In the eighteenth century, the insane were treated with great harshness. A theology student-turned-physician, Philippe Pinel became interested in their cause when a friend went insane, rushed into a forest, and was devoured by wolves. Placed in charge of an asylum with six hundred inmates (as well as five thousand pensioners), Pinel developed innovative treatments that stressed kindness, hygiene, and work therapy. He took no sides in the French Revolution but tried to help those who were proscribed by it. During the 1822 anti-clerical riots at the École de Médecine, he was deprived of his professorship. It was never restored to him.

PERCIVALL POTT (1714–1788)

Notable in the field of clinical surgery, Percivall Pott described a particular type of ankle fracture (which he himself had experienced) known as "Pott's Fracture" and a tubercular form of curvature of the spine known as "Pott's Disease." He gave the first description of congenital hernia and was the first to link genital cancer to the trade of chimney sweep. For much of his life he served as assistant surgeon at St. Bartholomew's Hospital. There he gave lectures that were highly regarded in the profession. A lover of people, he practiced the commandment to love one's neighbor as oneself, devoting his entire life to service. The day before he died, he remarked, "My lamp is almost extinguished. I hope it has burned for others."

WILLIAM PROUT (1785–1850)

An M.D., William Prout also authored one of the Bridgewater Treatises in defense of the existence of God. Titled *Chemistry, Meteorology, and the Function of Digestion considered with Reference to Natural Theology*, it was an eminently forgettable work.

VICTOR RAMBO (1894–1987)

Victor Rambo was a missionary doctor to India, where he developed surgical techniques for restoring sight to the blind.

JOHN LAMBERT RICHMOND (1785–1855)

John Richmond, a frontier practitioner, performed the first recorded successful Caesarean delivery in the United States. On Sundays, this Baptist minister preached in the open air and in barns. He took menial jobs to support himself and his family. Working night and day to save lives during a cholera outbreak, he contracted the disease himself. Although he survived, he lived out his remaining years broken in body and spirit.

PETER MARK ROGET (1779–1869)

As compiler of his *Thesaurus,* Peter Mark Roget obtained lasting fame. In his own day, his Bridgewater Treatise in defense of the existence of God was considered his most enduring work. Roget was a physician of Huguenot extraction.

BENJAMIN RUSH (1746–1813)

Converted in the Great Awakening, Benjamin Rush held Christian beliefs all of his life. As a medical practitioner, his methods and theories were highly erroneous. However, his great concern for medical training made him one of the first medical educators in America, and he imparted to his students a high sense of concern for the patient. He was a pioneer in the study of mental disorders.

THEODOR SCHWANN (1810–1882)

The Roman Catholic Theodor Schwann is credited with formulating the theory of the cell, especially with regard to the nucleus, a work filled out by his associate Matthias Jakob Schleiden. Schwann passed up a professorship at Wurzburg because he distrusted the students' atheistic tendencies.

ALBERT SCHWEITZER (1875–1965)

Albert Schweitzer comes to mind when one thinks of the doctor as a missionary. The last third of his life was spent in the African jungles as a physician to the sick. He veered far from orthodox Christianity, believing that Christ was fallible and accepting a philosophy close to pantheism. All the same, he believed in the Resurrection.

SAMUEL SEABURY (1729–1796)
Although Samuel Seabury studied medicine at Edinburgh for two years, it was as a bishop of the Episcopal church in Connecticut that he had the most influence, laboring to retain a Christocentric Anglo-Catholic piety in the church. He insisted on keeping unedited the Apostles' Creed and resisted deletion of the Nicene Creed from the *Prayer Book.* His influence in New England was substantial.

GORDON S. SEAGRAVE (1897–1965)
Gordon S. Seagrave became internationally known as the author of *Burma Surgeon, My Hospital in the Hills,* and other accounts of his medical missionary work in Burma.

NICHOLAS STENO (1631–1686)
Nicholas Steno, the founder of the science of geology, became a Christian bishop. Among his many interests was anatomy; he discovered the parotid duct, which is sometimes named for him.

SYLVIUS (FRANCIS DE LA BÖE) (1614–1672)
Chief of the iatrochemists, Sylvius looked for chemical explanations for illness. He became one of the best-known medical teachers of his day, training, among others, the great Steno, the father of geology. Sylvius was a member of the despised Walloons (a Huguenot group) and treated their sick without fee.

THEODORIC DE LUCCA (1205–1298)
Had Theodoric de Lucca been heeded, medicine would have been a gentler, more healing art much sooner than it was. He disclaimed the notion of laudable pus, saying that cleanliness would reduce the likelihood of inflammation after surgery. During surgery, he used a mixture of opium and mandrake juice on a sponge held to the patient's nose as an anesthetic. He argued against using cauterization. A monk, Theodoric became a bishop.

ROBERT BENTLY TODD (1809–1860)

Robert Bently Todd was not only a famous physiologist and neurologist, but also one who believed strongly "that the religious and moral duties of a doctor are just as important as practical and scientific attainment." He did his utmost to instill religious principles into his students.

WILLIAM TUKE (1732–1822)

The Quaker William Tuke was unaware of the work of Philippe Pinel in France when he founded the York Retreat to care for members of the Society of Friends (Quakers) who had lost their ability to reason. He adopted exercise, work therapy, kind treatment, moral education, and Bible readings—essentially the same elements Pinel used. The Retreat was highly successful and widely imitated.

GERHARD VAN SWIETEN (1700–1772)

Because he was a Roman Catholic, Van Swieten was not permitted to fill Boerhaave's seat at the Protestant University of Leyden. Notable for his reforms of medical education and military medicine, he also played a leading part in creating the Vienna school of medicine and wrote a commentary on Boerhaave's aphorisms.

SIR CECIL P. G. WAKELEY (1892–1979)

An eminent surgeon, Wakeley served as surgeon rear admiral during World War II. He was president of a Bible league and of an evolution protest movement.

JOHANN WEYER (1512–1576)

Many people consider Johann Weyer to be the founder of modern psychiatry. A devout Lutheran, he was at the same time a physician, an innovator in gynecology, and a student of mental diseases. He labored to end the burning of "witches," discussing their symptoms as medical and psychological phenomena, although he firmly believed that many such people were dupes of Satan. In his opinion, the burning of witches disgraced Christianity. He frequently cited the Scriptures to make his points.

ROBERT WILLAN (1757–1812)

At John Fothergill's urging, Robert Willan began his practice in London. His work at a public dispensary brought him increasing recognition. Like his pupil Thomas Bateman, he was interested in skin diseases. Indeed, Bateman credited Willan's work as foundational to his own specialization in the field. Willan was so interested in the life of Christ that he compiled his own account from the four gospels.

THOMAS WILLIS (1621–1675)

Author of one of the Bridgewater Treatises in defense of faith, Thomas Willis is remembered for his advancement of our understanding of fevers and his comprehension of the structural purpose of *The Ring of Willis*, which ensures an uninterrupted blood supply to the brain. Willis conducted novel research showing that the souls of men and animals differ. These studies remain of residual value to psychology. A friend of Robert Boyle *(Boyle's Law of Gases)* and Christopher Wren (architect of St. Paul's Cathedral), Willis was an early member of the Royal Society.

JOHN WOODWARD (1665–1728)

Strongly creationist in his views and believing in the biblical account of the Flood, John Woodward contributed sound fieldwork to the science of geology and served as a professor of medicine at Gresham College.

THOMAS YOUNG (1773–1829)

Thomas Young is best remembered today as the first scientist to perform a double-slit experiment with light. He was also in the forefront in deciphering Egyptian hieroglyphs. As a medical professor and researcher, he advanced our knowledge of the eye, especially astigmatism. Originally a Quaker, he joined the Church of England.

Bibliography

GENERAL WORKS

Asimov, Isaac. *A Short History of Biology.* Garden City, N.Y.: Natural History Press, 1964.

————. *Asimov's Biographical Encyclopedia of Science and Technology.* New York: Doubleday, 1964.

Bernier, Paul. *Père Laval.* Rome: Congregation of the Holy Spirit, 1978.

Bettmann, Otto L. *History of Medicine.* Springfield, Ill.: Charles C. Thomas, 1956.

Curti, Merle. "Psychological Theories in American Thought." In *Dictionary of the History of Ideas,* Vol. 4. Edited by Philip P. Weiner. New York: Scribner's, 1973.

Dictionary of American Biography. New York: Scribner's, 1964.

Dictionary of National Biography. London: Oxford University, 1968.

Ehrenwald, Jan. *History of Psychotherapy: From Healing Magic to Encounter,* 205–8. New York: Jason Aronson, 1976.

Encyclopedia of American Biography. Edited by John A. Garraty and Jerome L. Sternstein. New York: Harper and Row, 1974.

Feldman, Anthony, and Peter Ford. *Scientists and Inventors.* New York: Facts on File, 1979.

Gillispie, Charles Coulston. *Genesis and Geology.* Cambridge, Mass., 1951.

Gillispie, Charles Coulston, ed. *Dictionary of Scientific Biography.* New York: Scribner's, 1970.

Haggard, Howard. *The Doctor in History.* New Haven: Yale, 1934.

Inglis, Brian. *A History of Medicine.* Cleveland: World, 1965.

Kennedy, James, and Jerry Newcombe. *What If Jesus Had Never Been Born?* Nashville: Thomas Nelson, 1994.

King, Lester S. *The Medical World of the 18th Century.* Chicago: University of Chicago, 1958.

Kunitz, Stanley J., and Howard Haycraft. *American Authors 1600–1900: A Biographical Dictionary of American Literature,* 664. New York: H. W. Wilson, 1938.

Lockyer, Herbert. *Last Words of Saints and Sinners.* Grand Rapids: Kregel, 1969.

Lyons, Albert S., and R. Joseph Petrucelli. *Medicine: An Illustrated History.* New York: Harry N. Abrams, 1987.

Marks, Geoffrey, and William K. Beatty. *The Story of Medicine in America,* 177, 294. New York: Scribner's, 1973.

McGrew, Roderick E. *Encyclopedia of Medical History.* New York: McGraw-Hill, 1985.

Morris, Henry M. *Men of Science, Men of God: Great Scientists Who Believed the Bible.* San Diego: Creation Life, 1982.

Nuland, Sherwin B. *Doctors; The Biography of Medicine.* New York: Knopf, 1988.

Osler, William. *The Evolution of Modern Medicine.* New Haven, Conn.: Yale University, 1921.

Rosen, George. *400 Years of a Doctor's Life.* New York: Schuman, ca. 1947.

Sigerist, Henry E. *The Great Doctors.* Garden City, N.Y.: Doubleday, 1958.

Silverberg, Robert. *The Great Doctors.* New York: Scholastic Book Services, 1964.

Singer, Charles. *A Short History of Scientific Ideas to 1900.* London: Oxford University, 1959.

Singer, Charles, and E. Ashworth Underwood. *A Short History of Medicine.* New York: Oxford, 1962.

Talbott, John H. *A Biographical History of Medicine: Excerpts and Essays on the Men and Their Work.* New York: Grune & Stratton, 1970.

Thornton, John L. *A Select Bibliography of Medical Biography.* London: The Library Association, 1970.

Trimpi, Helen P. "Witchcraft." In *Dictionary of the History of Ideas,* Vol. 4. Edited by Philip P. Weiner. New York: Scribner's, 1973.

Uglow, Jennifer. *Macmillan Dictionary of Women's Biography.* London: Macmillan, 1989.

Walsh, James J. *Old Time Makers of Medicine.* New York: Fordham University, 1911.

Wintle, Justin, ed. *Makers of 19th Century Culture, 1800–1914.* London: Routledge and Kegan Paul, 1982.

SIR CHARLES BELL

Bell, Charles. *The Hand: Its Mechanism and Vital Endowments as Evincing Design.* London: William Pickering, 1833.

Dictionary of National Biography. London: Oxford University, 1968.

Gordon-Taylor, Gordon, and E. W. Walls. *Sir Charles Bell: His Life and Times.* Edinburgh: E & S Livingstone, Ltd., 1958.

HERMANN BOERHAAVE

Gillispie, Charles Coulston, ed. *Dictionary of Scientific Biography.* New York: Scribner's, 1970.

Johnson, Samuel. "The Life of Dr. Hermann Boerhaave." In *Samuel Johnson.* Edited by Donald Green. The Oxford Authors Series. Oxford: Oxford University, 1984.

King, Lester S. *The Medical World of the 18th Century.* Chicago: University of Chicago, 1958.

Lindeboom, G. A. *Hermann Boerhaave: The Man and His Work.* London: Methuen and Co., 1968.

Sigerist, Henry E. *The Great Doctors.* Garden City, N.Y.: Doubleday, 1958.

PAUL & MARGARET BRAND

Brand, Paul. Letter to the author.

Brand, Paul, and Philip Yancy. *Fearfully and Wonderfully Made.* Grand Rapids: Zondervan, 1987.

———. *In His Image.* Grand Rapids: Zondervan, 1987.

———. *The Gift of Pain.* Grand Rapids: Zondervan, 1993.

Feeny, Patrick. *The Fight Against Leprosy.* London: Elek Books, 1964.

Martin, Betty. *Miracle at Carville.* New York: Doubleday and Co., 1953.

Wilson, Dorothy Clarke. *Ten Fingers for God.* New York: McGraw-Hill, 1965.

Yancy, Philip. "Paul Brand." In *Chosen Vessels: Portraits of Outstanding Christian Men.* Edited by Charles Turner. Ann Arbor, Mich.: Vine, 1985.

PAUL CARLSON

Anderson, Carl Philip, compiler. *There Was a Man . . . His Name: Paul Carlson.* Westwood, N.J.: Revell, 1965.

Carlson, Lois. *Monganga Paulo: The Congo Ministry and Martyrdom of Paul Carlson, M.D.* New York: Harper and Row, 1966.

Time. December 4, 1964.

JAMES DERHAM

Brawley, Benjamin. *Negro Builders and Heroes.* Chapel Hill, N.C.: University of North Carolina, 1937.

Morais, Herbert M. *The History of the Negro in Medicine.* International Library of Negro Life and History. New York: Publishers Co., 1967.

Williams, George W. *History of the Negro Race in America from 1619 to 1880.* New York: G. P. Putnam, 1883.

Woodson, Carter G. *Negro Makers of History.* Washington, D.C.: Associated Publishers, 1945.

FABIOLA

Butler, Alban. *Lives of the Saints.* New York: Kennedy, ca. 1956.

Kelly, J. N. D. *Jerome: His Life, His Writings, and Controversies.* London: Duckworth, 1975.

The New Catholic Encyclopedia. New York: McGraw-Hill, 1967.

Page, T. E.; E. Capps; and W. H. Rouse, eds. "Letter LXXVII." In *Select Letters of St. Jerome.* Translated by F. A. Wright. New York: Putnam, 1933.

Uglow, Jennifer. *Macmillan Dictionary of Women's Biography,* 2d ed. London: Macmillan, 1989.

JOHN FLYNN

Australian Dictionary of Biography. [Melbourne]: Melbourne University, 1981.

Idriess, Ion L. *Flynn of the Inland.* Sydney: Angus and Robertson, 1932.

McPheat, W. Scott. *John Flynn: Apostle to the Inland.* London: Hodder and Stroughton, 1963.

JOHN FOTHERGILL

Carner, Betsy C., and Christopher C. Booth. *Chain of Friendship.* Cambridge, Mass., 1971.

Dictionary of National Biography. London: Oxford University, 1968.

Fox, R. Hingston. *Dr. John Fothergill and His Friends: Chapters in an Eighteenth-Century Life.* London: Macmillan, 1919.

Herbst, Josephine. *New Green World.* New York: Hastings, 1954.

WILFRED GRENFELL

Dictionary of National Biography. London: Oxford University, 1968.

Garlick, Phyllis. *Six Great Missionaries.* London: Hamish Hamilton, 1955.

Grenfell, Wilfred. *A Labrador Doctor.* Boston: Houghton-Mifflin, 1919.

Kerr, J. Lennox. *Wilfred Grenfell: His Life and Work.* New York: Dodd, Mead & Co., 1959.

ALBRECHT VON HALLER

Edwards, Paul. *Encyclopedia of Philosophy.* New York: Free Press, 1967.

Encyclopedia of World Biography. Detroit: Gale, 1998.

Francke, Kuno. *A History of German Literature as Determined by Social Forces.* New York: Holt, 1913.

Garland, Henry and Mary Garland. *Oxford Companion to German Literature.* Oxford: Oxford University, 1986.

Gillispie, Charles Coulston, ed. *Dictionary of Scientific Biography.* New York: Scribner's, 1970.

Kunitz, Stanley J., and Vineta Colby. *European Authors, 1000–1900.* New York: H. W. Wilson, 1967.

Ritchie, James MacPherson. *Periods in German Literature.* Chester Springs, Pa.: Dufour, 1967.

Sigerist, Henry E. *The Great Doctors.* Garden City, N.Y.: Doubleday, 1958.

Talbott, John H. *A Biographical History of Medicine: Excerpts and Essays on the Men and Their Work.* New York: Grune and Stratton, 1970.

THOMAS HODGKIN

Dictionary of National Biography. London: Oxford University, 1968.

Hamilton, Bailey, and W. J. Bishop. *Notable Names in Medicine and Surgery.* London: H. K. Lewis, 1959.

Talbott, John H. *A Biographical History of Medicine: Excerpts and Essays on the Men and Their Work.* New York: Grune and Stratton, 1970.

EDWARD JENNER

Allen, John. *One Hundred Great Lives.* New York: Journal of Living, 1944.

Dictionary of National Biography. London: Oxford University, 1968.

Eberle, Irmengarde. *Edward Jenner and Smallpox Vaccination.* New York: Watts, 1962.

Gillispie, Charles Coulston, ed. *Dictionary of Scientific Biography.* New York: Scribner's, 1970.

Jenner, Edward. "An Inquiry into the Causes and Effects of the Variolae Vaccinal, or Cowpox." In *Treasury of World Science.* Edited by Dagobert D. Runes. New York: Philosophical Library, 1962.

Sigerist, Henry E. *The Great Doctors.* Garden City, N.Y.: Doubleday, 1958.

Silverberg, Robert. *The Great Doctors.* New York: Scholastic Book Services, 1964.

HOWARD ATWOOD KELLY

Capper, W. Melville. *Some Great Christian Doctors.* London: Tyndale, 1960.

Davis, Audrey W. *Dr. Kelly of Hopkins.* Baltimore: Johns Hopkins, 1959.

Kelly, Howard A. *A Scientific Man and the Bible: A Personal Testimony.* New York: Harper, 1925.

THOMAS STORY KIRKBRIDE

Cherry, Charles L. *A Quiet Haven: Quakers, Moral Treatment, and Asylum Reform.* Rutherford: Fairleigh University, 1989.

Dictionary of American Biography. New York: Scribner's, 1964.

Kirkbride, Thomas S. *On the Construction, Organization, and General Arrangements of Hospitals for the Insane.* New York: Arno, 1973.

Morton, Thomas G., assisted by Frank Woodbury. *The History of the Pennsylvania Hospital, 1751–1895.* Philadelphia: Times Printing House, 1895.

Tomes, Nancy. *A Generous Confidence: Thomas Story Kirkbride and the Art of Asylum Keeping, 1840–1883.* Cambridge: Cambridge University, 1984.

C. EVERETT KOOP

Barrett, Eric C., and David Fisher. *Scientists Who Believe: 21 Tell Their Own Stories.* Chicago: Moody, 1984.

Koop, C. Everett. *Koop: The Memoirs of America's Family Doctor.* New York: Random House, 1991.

Minnery, Tom, ed. *Pornography: A Human Tragedy.* Wheaton, Ill: Christianity Today and Tyndale House, 1986.

Reagan, Ronald. *Abortion and the Conscience of the Nation.* Nashville: Nelson, 1984.

RENÉ THÉOPHILE HYACINTHE LAËNNEC

Gillispie, Charles Coulston, ed. *Dictionary of Scientific Biography.* New York: Scribner's, 1970.

Kervran, Roger. *Laënnec: His Life and Times.* New York: Pergamon, 1960.

Nuland, Sherwin B. *Doctors: The Biography of Medicine.* New York: Knopf, 1988.

Sigerist, Henry E. *The Great Doctors.* Garden City, N.Y.: Doubleday, 1958.

Talbott, John H. *A Biographical History of Medicine: Excerpts and Essays on the Men and Their Work.* New York: Grune and Stratton, 1970.

JOHN COAKLEY LETTSOM

Abraham, James Johnston. *Lettsom: His Life, Times, Friends and Descendants.* London: William Heinemann, 1933.

Dictionary of National Biography. London: Oxford University, 1968.

Fox, R. Hingston. *Dr. John Fothergill and His Friends: Chapters in an Eighteenth-Century Life.* London: Macmillan, 1919.

Power, D'Arcy. *British Masters of Medicine.* Freeport, N.Y.: Books for Libraries, 1969.

JOSEPH LISTER

Allen, John. *One Hundred Great Lives.* New York: Journal of Living, 1944.

Capper, W. Melville. *Some Great Christian Doctors.* London: Tyndale, 1960.

Dictionary of National Biography. London: Oxford University, 1968.

Lister, Joseph. "On the Antiseptic Principle of the Practice of Surgery." In *Treasury of World Science,* 642–653. Edited by Dagobert D. Runes. New York: Philosophical Library, 1962.

Noble, Iris. *The Courage of Doctor Lister.* New York: Messner, 1960.

Nuland, Sherwin B. *Doctors: The Biography of Medicine.* New York: Knopf, 1988.

Sigerist, Henry E. *The Great Doctors.* Garden City, N.Y.: Doubleday, 1958.

Silverberg, Robert. *The Great Doctors.* New York: Scholastic Book Services, 1964.

Wrench, G. T. *Lord Lister: His Life and Work.* London: T. Fisher Unwin, 1913.

LUKE

Aspland, Alfred. *The Four Evangelists.* Manchester: The Holbien Society, 1873.

Barclay, William. *The Gospel of Luke.* Philadelphia: Westminster, 1975.

Butler, Alban. *Lives of the Saints.* New York: Kennedy [ca. 1956].

The New Catholic Encyclopedia. New York: McGraw-Hill, 1967.

Fitzmeyer, Joseph A. *The Gospel According to Luke.* Anchor Bible. Garden City, New York: Doubleday and Co., 1986.

Munck, Johannes. *The Acts of the Apostles.* Anchor Bible. Garden City, New York: Doubleday and Co., 1986.

Tenney, Merrill C., gen. ed. *Pictorial Bible Dictionary.* Nashville: Southwestern Company, 1972.

Ramsay, W. M. *Luke the Physician and Other Studies in the History of Religion.* Grand Rapids: Baker, 1956.

Scott, John A. *Luke: Greek Physician and Historian,* Evanston, Ill.: Northwestern University, 1930.

Walsh, James A. "St. Luke the Physician," appendix to *Old Time Makers of Medicine.* New York: Fordham University Press, 1911.

JAMES PAGET

Byock, Jesse L. "Paget's Disease." In *Scientific American.* January, 1995, 86.

Capper, W. Melville. *Some Great Christian Doctors.* London: Tyndale, 1960.

Dictionary of National Biography. London: Oxford University, 1968.

Rosen, George. *400 Years of a Doctor's Life.* New York: Schuman, ca. 1947.

Talbott, John H. *A Biographical History of Medicine: Excerpts and Essays on the Men and Their Work.* New York: Grune and Stratton, 1970.

AMBROISE PARÉ

Gillispie, Charles Coulston, ed. *Dictionary of Scientific Biography.* New York: Scribner's, 1970.

Nuland, Sherwin B. *Doctors: The Biography of Medicine.* New York: Knopf, 1988.

Paget, Stephen. *Ambroise Paré and His Times, 1510–1590.* New York: Putnam, 1897.

Paré, Ambroise. "Journeys in Diverse Places." In *Treasury of World Science.* Edited by Dagobert D. Runes. New York: Philosophical Library, 1962.

Sigerist, Henry E. *The Great Doctors.* Garden City, N.Y.: Doubleday, 1958.

Silverberg, Robert. *The Great Doctors.* New York: Scholastic Book Services, 1964.

JAMES RAMSAY

Dictionary of National Biography. London: Oxford University, 1968.

Pollock, John. *Victims of the Long March and Other Stories.* Waco, Tex.: Word, 1970.

Shyllon, Folarin. *James Ramsay: The Unknown Abolitionist.* Edinburgh: Canongate, 1977.

WALTER REED

Capper, W. Melville. *Some Great Christian Doctors.* London: Tyndale Press, 1960.

Dictionary of American Biography. New York: Scribner's, 1964.

Gillispie, Charles Coulston, ed. *Dictionary of Scientific Biography.* New York: Scribner's, 1970.

Higgins, Helen Boyd. *Walter Reed: The Boy Who Wanted to Know.* New York: Bobbs-Merrill, 1958.

Kelly, Howard Atwood. *Walter Reed and Yellow Fever.* Baltimore: Medical Standard Book Co., 1906.

Wood, Laura Newbold. *Walter Reed: Doctor in Uniform.* New York: Messner, 1943.

Silverberg, Robert. *The Great Doctors.* New York: Scholastic Book Services, 1964.

SIR JOHN RICHARDSON

Dictionary of National Biography. London: Oxford University, 1968.

Johnson, Robert E. *Sir John Richardson: Arctic Explorer, Natural Historian, Naval Surgeon.* London: Taylor and Francis, 1976.

Levere, Trevor H. *Science and the Canadian Arctic; A Century of Exploration.* Cambridge: Cambridge University, 1993.

SIR RONALD ROSS

Dictionary of National Biography. London: Oxford University, 1968.

Gillispie, Charles Coulston, ed. *Dictionary of Scientific Biography.* New York: Scribner's, 1970.

Kruif, Paul de. *Microbe Hunters.* New York: Pocket Books, 1943.

Mégroz, R. L. *Ronald Ross: Discoverer and Creator.* London: G. Allen and Unwin, 1931.

IDA SCUDDER

Garlick, Phyllis. *Six Great Missionaries.* London: Hamish Hamilton, 1955.

"Ida S. Scudder." http://vellorecmc.org/scudder.html

Jeffery, Mary Pauline. *Ida S. Scudder of Vellore: The Life Story of Ida Sophia Scudder.* Mysore, India: J. Brown, 1951.

Wilson, Dorothy Clarke. *Dr. Ida: The Story of Dr. Ida Scudder of Vellore.* New York: McGraw-Hill, 1959.

ARTHUR RENDLE SHORT

Capper, William A. *Arthur Rendle Short: Surgeon and Christian.* London: InterVarsity, 1955.

Short, A. Rendle. *Modern Discovery and the Bible.* London: InterVarsity Fellowship, 1949.

JAMES YOUNG SIMPSON

Allen, John. *One Hundred Great Lives.* New York: Journal of Living, 1944.

Dictionary of National Biography. London: Oxford University, 1968.

Gordon, H. Liang. *Sir James Young Simpson and Chloroform.* London: T. Fisher Unwin, 1897.

NATHAN SMITH

Dictionary of American Biography. New York: Scribner's, 1964.

Knight, J. "An Eulogium on Nathan Smith, M.D., Late Professor of the Theory and Practice of Physic and Surgery in the Medical Institution of Yale College, Pronounced at His Funeral by J. Knight, M.D., Professor of Anatomy and Physiology." *Bibliotheca Americana.* New Haven: H. Howe, 1829. Microform.

Smith, Emily. *Nathan Smith.* New Haven, Conn.: Yale University Press, 1914.

CLARA SWAIN

Encyclopedia of World Methodism. Nashville: United Methodist Publishing House, 1974.

Houghton, Rev. Ross C. *Women of the Orient: An Account of the Religious Intellectual and Social Condition of Women.* Cincinnati: Walden and Stowe, 1877.

Kaufman, Martin; Stuart Galishoff; and Todd Savitt, eds. *Dictionary of American Medical Biography.* Westport, Conn.: Greenwood, 1984.

Swain, Clara. *A Glimpse of India.* New York: Garland, 1987 (facsimile of 1909 edition).

THOMAS SYDENHAM

Capper, W. Melville. *Some Great Christian Doctors.* London: Tyndale, 1960.

Dewhurst, Kenneth. *Dr. Thomas Sydenham: His Life and Original Writings.* London: Wellcome Historical Medical Library, 1966.

Dictionary of National Biography. London: Oxford University, 1968.

Power, D'Arcy. *British Masters of Medicine.* Freeport, N.Y.: Books for Libraries, 1969.

Sigerist, Henry E. *The Great Doctors.* Garden City, N.Y.: Doubleday, 1958.

PAUL WHITE

Gale Research Co. *Contemporary Authors. New Revision Series.* Detroit: Gale Publishing, 1988.

White, Paul. *Alias Jungle Doctor.* Exeter, England: Paternoster, 1977.

_____. *Doctor of Tanganyika.* Grand Rapids: Eerdmans, 1955.

_____. *Get Moving; Motivation for Living.* Sydney: Anzea Books, 1983.

——. *Jungle Doctor's Fables*. Chicago: Moody, 1971.

White, Ruth. Letters to the author.

Who's Who in Australia. Melbourne: Herald, 1980.

[Some Paul White titles are available in the United States from OM Literature, P.O. Box 1047, Waynesboro GA, 30830-2047.]

Index

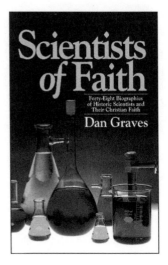